Spring Flowers

KARIN GREINER

Series Editor:
LESLEY YOUNG

MEREHURST

Introduction

Each year, as if to signal the end of winter, the arrival in our gardens of delicate snowdrops, graceful narcissi and bright crocuses announces that spring is here again! The first glimpses of spring colour in the garden or balcony tubs is, however, just a faint shadow of the splendour that spring is about to present to us. With a little imagination, you can make full use of the beauty and variety of the huge range of spring flowers to clothe your garden, balcony or patio with colour. This guide will help you to choose the ideal plants for you by providing information on a selection of enchanting plants with easy-to-follow tips on their care. Plant expert Karin Greiner explains the correct way to plant spring flowers, how to care for them and how they can be propagated. Colour photographs introduce many of the most beautiful plants, among them the ever-popular bulbs and colourful perennials, many of which are ideal for a wild garden. Detailed instructions on care, as well as an overview of planting times in autumn and spring, will ensure that everything flourishes and blooms both inside your house and out in the garden from the last month of winter through to the first month of summer. Planting ideas for flowerbeds, borders, lawns, balcony boxes, pots and bowls will enable you to make the most of spring with hardly any effort. In addition, there are tips on planting combinations using your favourite colours.

Contents

4 **All about spring flowers**
Nature awakes

4 Spring flowers in myth and legend
4 The star among spring flowers
6 Growth and botany

Pheasant's eye (Adonis vernalis).

8 **Planting, care and propagation**
A place in the sun

8 The right position
9 Tips on laying out your garden
10 Planting
12 Fertilizing
12 Watering
12 Pruning and deadheading
14 Dying back
15 Lifting and storing bulbs and tubers
15 Winter protection
16 Propagation
18 Spring flowers indoors

19 **Pests and diseases**
Healthy plants develop immunity

19 Promoting natural immunity
19 Common problems of bulbous plants
19 Plant protection agents
19 Animal pests
20 Mice, voles and rabbits
20 Blackbirds and sparrows
20 Slugs and snails
20 Thrips and nematodes
20 Biological sprays
21 Fungal diseases
21 Common diseases of bulbous and tuberous plants
22 Viral and bacterial diseases

24 **Spring flowers in balcony boxes**
Splendour on your balcony

24 Tips on choosing plants
24 How long will flowers last in a spring tub?
25 Spacing of plants
26 The balcony
28 Planting times: autumn and spring
28 Choosing colours for your balcony

Parrot tulip.

Christmas roses (Helleborus niger) are among the first harbingers of spring.

The author
Karin Greiner is a biologist with a special interest in ecology. She has worked at the Institute for Botanical-Ecological Advice in Munich since 1984 and has published numerous papers on gardening topics, in particular on bulbous and tuberous plants. She is an expert on garden design, specializing in wild gardens, with particular emphasis on maintaining environmental stability.

Acknowledgements
The author and publishers wish to thank Angelika Weber of the Institute for Botanical-Ecological Advice for her invaluable and practical comments on the original text.

Important: Please read the Author's Note on page 63.

29 Flowers on the balcony all spring long
30 Care after flowering
30 Overwintering balcony boxes

32 **Recommended species and varieties**
Flowering magic in spring

34 Tulips
36 Narcissi
38 Crocuses
40 Fritillaries
42 The first signs of spring
42 Snowdrops
43 Winter aconite
43 Snowflakes
44 Hyacinths
46 Blue spring-flowering plants
48 Irises

50 Spring rarities
52 Sun-loving herbaceous perennials
54 Shade-loving herbaceous perennials
56 Cushion-forming herbaceous perennials
58 Biennial spring-flowering plants
58 Forget-me-nots
59 Wallflowers
59 Pansies
59 Daisies

60 **Index**

63 **Author's note**

All about spring flowers

Nature awakes

Garden crocus.

No other season creates such feelings of hope as spring. After the endless gloomy, grey skies of winter, the awakening of nature seems like a miracle: the shoots of bulbous plants and hardy perennials seem to appear from nowhere and, over the span of a few weeks, will turn your garden into a sea of colour.

Even by late winter some spring shoots are beginning to reach out towards the first, warming rays of the sun. Snowdrops and crocuses announce the arrival of spring in gardens and on balconies. At first, only a few flowers unfold their petals but soon the entire neighbourhood appears to explode into an incomparable firework display of shapes and colours. By the time the tulip blossoms are slowly fading and the apple trees are in full bloom, spring is already coming to an end.

Spring flowers in myth and legend
No other group of plants is so surrounded by myths, fairy tales and legends as spring flowers. Their names are associated with countless stories in folklore.
The narcissus received its name in Ancient Greece and is featured in one of the legends of Greek mythology. This plant, which likes to grow on the banks of a pond or stream, bears the name of a Greek youth called Narcissus who thought himself to be quite beautiful. One

day, Narcissus was bending over a pool, enchanted by the sight of his own reflection in the water. When he reached out to embrace the image, he fell in and drowned. Vanity and self-obsession were his downfall. However, the gods took pity on him and transformed his dead body into a narcissus plant, which still casts its lovely reflection on the water even today.
The wild cowslip (*Primula veris*) is one of the first wild flowers of spring. Its charming umbels are reminiscent of the golden keys to the heavenly gates carried by St Peter. According to legend, St Peter opens the gates every spring and, such is his joy at the sight of all the new life, that he drops his keys which fall to Earth. There they are transformed into golden flowers which keep on blooming as if St Peter never again wishes to close the gates of Heaven after the harsh days of winter.
"Forget-me-not!" say the sky blue flowers of the plant of the same name just as the spring is coming to an end again. As a symbol of fidel-

ity, the forget-me-not (*Myosotis*) represents the hope of humankind that spring will return again next year.

The star among spring flowers
In past times, many spring flowers were considered to be very precious by the peoples of central Europe. Tulips, in particular, have a quite spectacular history. The ancestors of our garden tulips originated from Asia Minor and the Near East where, centuries ago, they were highly prized in palace gardens. The first tulips were purchased by the aristocracy of Central Europe as exotic gems treasured by the Moguls, Indian rulers in the sixteenth century. Soon these exotic plants were flowering in the gardens of the west. The great enthusiasm engendered for this unusual flower led raisers to experiment with new shapes and colours. In the Netherlands, in particular, still the leading country for tulips, a form of "tulip mania" broke out at the beginning of the seventeenth century, when a single bulb could be worth a small fortune. The tulip became an object of market speculation until legislation and an overabundance of tulips finally caused the market to collapse.
There is scarcely another spring flower that offers such a wealth of shape and colour as the tulip. Of some 4,000 possible varieties, only a few hundred are still on the market. Every year new cultivars are introduced, most of which soon disappear again. Few new introductions manage to assert themselves against the old, well-tried and much loved varieties.

Crocuses are an excellent source of nectar for honey bees (Apis mellifera).

Botany

A basic knowledge of botany is one of the tools of every successful gardener. If you are familiar with the natural growth processes of the plants you choose, you will be able to avoid mistakes when you are caring for them.

Survival strategies among spring flowers

Plants have developed various techniques for survival in unfavourable climatic conditions.

Biennial herbaceous plants, like pansies and wallflowers, have extended their growth cycle to cover two years. During the first year they conserve their energies and then flower and produce seeds during the second year. If the seeds of such plants are sown in summer, many will grow into strong, healthy plants by the autumn and will bear masses of flowers the following spring. Many biennials are still capable of producing flowers for several more years but the flowers become increasingly sparse, so it is usual to discard them after their first flowering and sow fresh seed.

NB: Annual plants do not produce flowers in spring as their development always begins in spring.

Herbaceous perennials

(Illustration 1)

Perennials are resilient plants whose above-ground parts often die down every year. The rootstock survives in the soil and the plant renews itself from its shoots. Among the early-flowering herbaceous perennials are aubrieta, bleeding heart (*Dicentra* spp.) and primulas.

Bulbs and tubers are also considered to be perennials which have developed special, underground storage organs to ensure their survival through difficult times. When climatic conditions are right, new plants will grow from the bulbs and tubers.

Bulbs

(Illustration 2)

Bulbs consist of several fleshy layers which enclose the part out of which the shoot, leaf and flower will develop and which supply the developing plant with sustenance. The outer skin, which is tough and dry, protects the bulb from drying out and from damage. Roots grow from the bottom of the bulb.

Tubers

(Illustration 3)

Tubers are the "larders" of plants and are formed out of roots or shoots. They form more or less homogeneous masses, surrounded by a tough, protective layer. Tubers come in different shapes:

● In root tubers (e.g. anemone), the swollen roots are bunched together like claws.

● Shoot tubers (e.g. winter aconite) are usually fat and rounded. The new shoots grow out of the "eyes".

The bulb tuber is an in-between form, in which the fleshy scales fuse into a firm, lumpy mass, with roots sprouting in a crown. There are round bulb tubers or longish ones (bulbous iris).

The life cycle of bulbous plants

(Illustration 4)

The example of the tulip can be used to demonstrate the life cycle of a bulbous plant. The cycle of the tuberous plants is very similar.

1. Herbaceous perennials like this cowslip will flower for many years.

2. Bulbs are underground storage organs.

Around the second month of autumn, the bulb, now in its dormant phase, is planted in the soil. A month later, a hard shoot tip will form, which is capable of piercing through quite compact layers of soil in spring. At the same time, roots begin to grow out of the

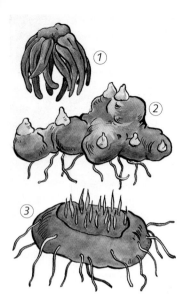

3. **Tubers:** 1. anemone; 2. winter aconite; 3. cyclamen.

base. These take over the function of water supply and also provide nourishment to the plant. Protected by the soil, the tulip survives the winter in this state.

Around the first and second months of spring, increasing warmth and moisture trigger the further development of the plant. By about six months after planting, the tulip will have produced fully developed leaves and flowers which have been sustained by the stored nutrients. The bulb itself shrinks more and more. Before it disappears completely, however, new little bulbils will begin to form in the axils of the innermost segments. These new bulbs will ensure the growth of new plants the following year.

The foliage will continue to store reserve nutrients for quite a long period after flowering is over. These substances will provide the necessary energy for new bulbs to form.

Finally, after a further three months, in late summer, the entire development cycle is completed and the new bulbs enter a dormant phase.

Botanical names

The common names of many flowers are often confusing and may even be different in different regions of a single country. For example, people in different areas often confuse the names snowdrop and snowflake, or bluebell and harebell. A plant can only be classified properly by the use of an official botanical name which provides information about its relationships to other plants of the same type and its special characteristics. Each plant has its own first and second name: a genus name and a species name.

The genus name is the first part of the name. It is written in italic script, with an uppercase (capital) letter, and is often the same for several closely related plants. For example, *Tulipa* is the generic name for all tulips.

The species name is the second name and is always written in italic script, with a lowercase (small) letter, for example, *Tulipa kaufmanniana*.

The variety name (if there is one) is a third name that is given to the plant by the raiser of that particular garden variety. It is enclosed in quotation marks. It often describes an important characteristic of the variety, for example, "The First".

NB: When speaking of "botanical" species, we usually mean wild species and their descendants. For example, "botanical crocuses" are all wild crocus species and the varieties bred from them, except for the large garden crocuses (*Crocus vernus*).

My tip: When choosing plants, take note of their botanical names. This is the only way to ensure that you have bought the right species. Variety names are important if you are looking for a particular cultivar, for example, a tulip of a special colour or petal formation.

4. **Growth cycle of a bulbous plant:** The growth cycle from planting through flowering to the formation of bulbs takes nine months.

Planting, care and propagation

A place in the sun

Flower bulbs.

The warm rays of the sun are needed to coax spring flowers out of their winter sleep, so it is no wonder that so few of them flourish in shady places. If you take account of the position required by such plants, you will be able to save a lot of time and effort.

The right position
Even with the best care, a plant will display feeble growth if it is planted in the wrong place. When choosing a position for your plants, it is a good idea to consider the prevailing conditions of the site. You must look at all the external influences that will interact around the plant. Among these are light, warmth, moisture and type of soil.

Light and warmth
Most spring flowers prefer positions in full sunlight or mostly sunny positions which also receive plenty of warmth. Warmth is the single most significant trigger for growth following the cold winter period. Cooler positions, which are generally shadier, are only suitable for a few plants with special requirements, like the Christmas rose (*Helleborus niger*) or *Hepatica nobilis*. (For the individual requirements of many popular spring flowers, see pp. 32-59.) Many spring-flowering plants are quite happy planted under deciduous trees and bushes. As the trees are still bare in the springtime,

sunlight can easily penetrate to the ground beneath. The spring flowers will have finished blooming by the time the leaves start appearing.

Moisture
The right degree of moisture is particularly important for bulbous and tuberous plants.
Sufficient moisture is essential *in the spring*, during the plants' main growth phase. If there is not enough rain, they will need watering.
In the summer, on the other hand, bulbous and tuberous plants require dry soil so that their underground parts can ripen properly. If they are in constantly wet positions during summer, they will tend to decay.

My tip: When you plant bulbs etc., insert a water-permeable drainage layer (see p. 26). Water-sensitive species can be protected with a sheet of polythene if there are long periods of wet weather.

The right kind of soil
Light to medium-heavy, neutral soils which are water permeable are optimal for tuberous and bulbous plants (which make up the larger percentage of spring flowers). A few spring flowers require acid or lime-rich soils (see pp. 32-59). Soils that are too light or too heavy can be treated before planting (see planting, p. 10).

Checking the soil
The following factors are important:
Consistency: Determining the consistency of your garden soil is quite simple. Take a handful of soil and crumble it between your fingers. The following rules apply:
● Light soil is sandy and will trickle through your fingers.
● Medium-heavy soil is loose and crumbly.
● Heavy soil is full of clay and can be squeezed into a sticky ball.

pH factor (degree of acidity): You can measure the pH value of your garden soil with the help of simple measuring devices. Various products are on sale in the gardening trade at reasonable prices.
● neutral soil has a pH value of 6.5-7.5;
● acid soil has a pH value of less than 6.5;
● alkaline soil has a pH value of more than 7.5.

My tip: You can send soil samples away to be analysed (enquire at your local garden centre).

Looking good together: *Cyclamineus narcissi, double tulips and Brodiaea laxa.*

Tips on laying out your garden
Spring flowers can brighten any part of the garden with their glowing colours. Their own particular shape of growth and flower arrangement will determine where they will look best. The more splendid, dominant types will be most effective in flowerbeds and borders, while plants with small flowers do better under a group of trees or bushes or in a rockery. There follow some recommendations for the positioning of different species of spring flowers.

For shrubberies: garden tulips, garden narcissi, hyacinths, fritillary, ranunculus, leopard's bane, primroses and bergenia.
In the rockery: botanical tulips, botanical narcissi, crocuses, fritillary, winter aconite, grape hyacinths, irises, dog's tooth violet, cyclamen, pheasant's eye, pasque flowers, primroses, all cushion-forming perennials.
Under trees or bushes: species of narcissus, crocuses, snowdrops, winter aconite, snowflakes, glory of the snow, scilla, anemones,

Ornithoganum, snake's head fritillary, bleeding heart, Christmas rose, Caucasian forget-me-not, violets.
Along the edge of a pond or stream: narcissi, snowflakes, marsh marigolds (king cups).
For the lawn, meadow or wild garden: *Crocus tomasinianus* and other botanical crocuses, glory of the snow, snake's head fritillary, snowdrops, grape hyacinths, Poeticus narcissi, scilla and Kaufmann tulips.

Planting

What kind of things should one watch out for when buying spring plants? When and where should they be planted?

Tips on buying

Only choose species and varieties of spring-flowering plants that you know are going to be suitable for the conditions that prevail in your garden (see pp. 32-59). Always check that the colours and shapes of the flowers you are about to buy will look right with the existing plants in your garden.

Bulbs and tubers: The larger the girth of the bulb or tuber, the larger the flowers (and the price). Good plants should be undamaged, compact and firm, without signs of disease (soft or discoloured places) and should not be dried up. The overall appearance of the plant should be healthy.

Perennial herbaceous plants:
These are most often sold as pot or container plants. They should look well developed and have several strong, healthy shoots. The roots should not be growing out of the pot and the soil should be free of weeds.
Warning: Some spring flowers are toxic. Make sure you read the relevant notes on pages 32-59!

Preparing the soil

Loosen up the soil in the places where you intend to plant (depth of plants, see p. 11) and remove all weeds, stones and old roots. Improve the soil with mature garden compost. Loosen up heavy soil by adding and mixing in sand. Conversely, very light soil can be improved by the addition of some loam to hold it together better.

Planting bulbs and tubers

Planting times: The species that flower in spring can be planted from late summer to mid-autumn. The best planting time is the first month of autumn. The earlier the bulbs are

2. *Drainage: Fill the bottom of the hole with sand or grit to form a flat mound.*

placed in the soil before the beginning of frosty weather, the more time they will have to settle and the better they will survive the winter. Species which need a relatively long time to form proper roots should be planted by the first month of autumn at the latest. This goes for snowdrops (*Galanthus*), snowflakes (*Leucojum*), narcissi (*Narcissus*), crocuses (*Crocus*), scilla (*Scilla*) and fritillaries (*Fritillaria*). All other species can still be planted as late as the second month of autumn.
NB: Bulbs and tubers should be bought just before they are planted to avoid unnecessary storage!
Tips on spring planting: Bulbous plants that have been brought on early by a gardener or in your own greenhouse, can be planted outside during the first and second months of spring as soon as the soil is no longer frozen. You can fill gaps in your flowerbeds or decorate a small, empty bed with these "forced" plants. The only drawback is that such a quick crop of beautiful flowers will cost much more.

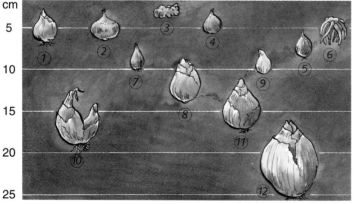

1. **Planting depths of some bulbous and tuberous plants:** *1. grape hyacinth; 2. crocus; 3. winter aconite; 4. snowdrop; 5. iris reticulata; 6. ranunculus; 7. botanical tulip; 8. garden tulip; 9. dog's tooth violet; 10. narcissus; 11. hyacinth; 12. fritillary (crown imperial).*

Planting depth
(Illustration 1)

General rule: Bulbs and tubers should be planted in the soil at a depth that equals three times their height. In light, sandy soils, the planting depth should be a little more, and in heavy soils a little less.

Spacing of plants: Plants need room to develop properly. Plant small bulbs/tubers (up to walnut size) about 5-8 cm (2-3 in) apart; larger bulbs 10-15 cm (4-6 in) apart.

Planting and drainage
(Illustration 2)

Large bulbs (larger than walnut size) should be planted further apart (make a separate hole for each one). Small bulbs can be planted with a special bulb dibber which creates a cylindrical hole that will accommodate two to three bulbs.

3. Planting bulbs in a basket: Ensure that the planting depth and spacing are correct.

My tip: Winter aconites, crocuses and other small tubers or bulbs that are to be planted in lawns or patches of grass, can be scattered randomly and then planted where they have fallen. This kind of distribution will appear more natural than deliberately planting them in groups.

Drainage: Bulbs do not thrive in waterlogged conditions, so you may need to insert a drainage layer to provide adequate drainage at the bottom of the planting hole.

● If the soil is light and loose, a flat, approximately finger-thick layer of sand beneath the bulbs will be sufficient.

● If the soil is very dense, very moist or heavy, the following procedure is recommended. Dig a hole about 5-10 cm (2-4 in) deeper than usual. Then scatter pebbles, fine gravel, broken pot shards or grit and sand in the hole. Place the bulbs on top of the drainage layer, then fill in the hole with soil and finish up by watering the bulbs well.

Planting bulbs in a basket
(Illustration 3)

Tulips, narcissi and other bulbs that have to be removed from the soil every few years can be placed in planting baskets. These flat baskets can later be removed from the soil quite easily, along with the bulbs they contain. The baskets thus facilitate digging up the bulbs and, at the same time, protect them against rodents. They can even be used for storage.

Perennial and biennial plants

Planting times: Plants bought in pots can be planted at any time during the vegetation phase of spring plants. Plants that are not in pots should be planted in early autumn, so that the roots will have time to spread out into the soil properly before the beginning of winter.

Planting depths: Perennials, biennials and bulbs should be planted at the same depth as they were in their pot. Planting them too deep

4. Plant shrubs at the same depth as before.

can lead to decay of the neck of the stem; planting them too shallow will cause them to dry up.

Spacing the plants: Perennials like bergenias, which take up quite a bit of space, will require more growth area than, for example, small forget-me-nots.

Correct spacing:
● small perennials 15-20 cm (6-8 in) apart;
● large perennials 25-40 cm (10-16 in) apart;
● cushion-forming perennials 25-35 cm (10-14 in) apart;
● biennials 15-20 cm (6-8 in) apart.

Planting
(Illustration 4)

Make the planting hole a little larger than the diameter of the rootstock, then loosen up the soil at the bottom of the hole. Set the plant in the hole, fill the hole with soil and press the rootstock down firmly. Water thoroughly.

Fertilizing

Plants need a balanced, well-regu-lated supply of nutrients to ensure their well-being. The most important plant nutrients are nitrogen, phos-phorous, potassium and lime, as well as trace elements such as manganese, zinc, iron, copper and magnesium. Depending on the type and consistency of the soil, such nutrients will be available in various amounts and concentrations. If your garden soil is of good quality, you will not need to worry about the nutrient supply as the soil will con-tain sufficient nutrients for the growth of plants for several years. When the plants no longer flourish, it is time to improve the soil, but it is necessary to give the matter some thought beforehand.

Soil analysis can provide accurate information about the nutrient con-tent of your soil (enquire about such a service at your local garden cen-tre). Before you use a fertilizer, take account of the specific nutritional needs of your plants, supply only those nutrients that are really need-ed and give them in the correct amounts.

Basic rule for fertilizing: Supplying too many nutrients is often more harmful than giving too few. Overfertilizing can lead to problems in growth development, sparse flowering, susceptibility to disease and a loss of hardiness. The best method is to enrich the soil with organic, natural substances before planting. This will eliminate the need to resort to mineral fertilizers that can be harmful to the environment.

The nutrient requirements of spring flowers

● Wild species, like botanical cro-cuses, *Scilla* or fritillaries, can man-age on few nutrients. Only really poor, nutrient-deficient soils will need to be improved for these species.

● Large tulips and narcissi, as well as short-lived biennials like pansies, are grateful for a plentiful supply of nutrients.

How to improve soil organically

Poorer soils should be treated with organic fertilizer before planting. Ripe garden compost or controlled-release fertilizer, like bone chips or bonemeal, should be sprinkled on, or mixed with, the soil. In the case of large planting areas, or if time is short, the soil can be covered with a thin layer of compost which will also serve as winter protection.

Fast fertilizing

In the case of poor soils and plants that need lots of nutrients, like gar-den tulips, the nutrient supply in the soil may be almost exhausted by the time of maximum growth. If you were not able to treat the soil beforehand with organic fertilizer, you can resort to fast-acting fertiliz-ers which will provide an instant supply of nutrients for the plants. In addition to mineral fertilizers, organ-ic, fast-dissolving and liquid fertiliz-ers are all available (such as nettle brew or a liquid fertilizer made from turnips).

Warning: Before using commercial fertilizers, read the instructions thor-oughly and avoid overdosing! Just like mineral fertilizers, ordinary gar-den compost and other organic fer-tilizers can also have a harmful effect if the doses are too large or are applied too often. Overfertilizing is detrimental to the soil and pol-lutes the ground water. All responsi-ble gardeners should realize that they have a duty to make only spar-ing use of fertilizers in order to pre-vent unnecessary damage to the environment.

Warning: Make sure that fertilizers are stored in a place that is inac-cessible to children and pets.

Watering

Water requirements will vary depending on the time of year and the developmental stage of the plants.

After planting, thorough watering is particularly important so that the plants get a good start.

In spring, spring-flowering plants need larger amounts of water, as do all plants at the time of their most rapid growth and flower for-mation. Usually, however, there is already plenty of water in the soil during spring, following the rainfall of winter. As soon as the soil dries out, however, you will have to start watering.

In summer, during their dormant phase, spring-flowering bulbous or tuberous plants will require only a little water. It is more important to avoid waterlogging at this time (moisture, see p. 8).

Herbaceous perennials will require plenty of water, even in summer.

Pruning and deadheading

The removal of faded flowerheads is not a sign of exaggerated tidiness but – depending on the species of plant – a very necessary gardening technique.

In the case of *garden varieties* of tulips, narcissi, hyacinths and some perennials (see pp. 32-59), the removal of faded flowers is benefi-cial to the plants as it prevents the formation of seeds, which would use up the plant's energy unneces-sarily. Make a point of deadheading the flowers as soon as they fade.

A romantic corner of the garden with Darwin tulips and forget-me-nots under a blossoming cherry tree.

The pure white flowers of the snowflake (Leucojum vernum) stand out against the dark, wintry soil.

In the case of **wild species** that are left to grow naturally, the formation of seed is desirable as it will ensure prolific propagation. There is no need to remove dead flowers from these plants.

In the case of **cushion-forming perennials**, cutting back will rejuvenate them. After flowering, cut all shoots back by about a third. Use a large pair of scissors to cut the entire cushion into shape. The plants will then form plenty of new shoots and remain compact without becoming bare in the centre.

Dying back

Many spring flowers seem to vanish completely by early summer. First the foliage turns yellow, then, over time, the leaves disappear completely. Only the underground organs of the plant remain viable. This process is called dying back.

Perennials: Make sure to mark the positions of plants that die back early, like bleeding heart (*Dicentra spectabilis*), pheasant's eye and pasque flowers, so that you can avoid damaging their roots when digging. The gaps above ground will soon be filled by later-flowering neighbouring plants.

Bulbs and tubers: Even though the slowly withering foliage is not very attractive, it should not be removed until it is completely yellow or dried out. With the help of these leaves, bulbous and tuberous plants build up important reserves of vital nutrients which are then held in underground storage organs to provide energy for the next year's growth.

NB: Lawns that contain bulbous plants should not be mowed until the end of spring or in the first month of summer.

My tip: The skilled planting of species that produce plenty of fast growing foliage will help to hide the fading leaves of narcissi and tulips.

Lifting and storing bulbs and tubers

You can remove the bulbs and tubers from the flowerbeds if you wish to make room for summer plants. The following points should, however, be noted.

Make sure the *foliage has dried up and turned completely yellow* before carefully lifting the bulbs or tubers out of the soil with a garden fork. Foliage that has not yet withered can now be cut off. Remove any loose soil from the bulbs or tubers and allow them to dry off in a shady place for a few days. Diseased or damaged bulbs and tubers, or those that are too small, should be discarded.

If the foliage is still upright but you need the space for new plants, the removed plants must be given an opportunity to complete their cycle in another position. Remove the bulbs or tubers from the soil, together with the foliage, and lay them out in a shady place in the garden. Cover the bulbs with loose soil and leave them to "rest" until the foliage has withered.

Storage

After lifting the bulbs and tubers, it is important to store them properly before replanting them in the autumn. If they are left out of soil for a long time, they risk drying out or becoming infested with fungi and moulds.

Proper storage: You will need a wooden box or tray. Cover the bottom of the box with a layer of peat, sawdust or wood shavings.

The bulbs/tubers should be laid loosely on this layer (they should not touch) and covered with another layer. Keep the box in a cool, dry, dark place (e.g. a cellar) until replanting time in autumn.

NB: *Fritillaria* and *Erythronia* spp. do not have a protective layer of skin around their bulbs, so they can only be stored in moist peat or some similar medium for a short time.

My tip: New bulbs or tubers should not be bought until shortly before you intend planting, to avoid unnecessary storage.

Warning: Make sure children or pets do not eat bulbs or tubers! Some of them are toxic (see pp. 32-59) and most can cause severe health problems.

Winter protection

Many species of bulbs and tubers originate from mountainous regions that are covered by a protective layer of snow during the winter. In regions with little or no snowfall, such species may sometimes be damaged by frost. Sensitive species, like jonquils, *Narcissus bulbocodium* and some *Fritillaria*, will need some form of winter protection. The same goes for cushion-forming plants, sensitive perennials like bleeding heart (*Dicentra spectabilis*) and many biennials. All newly planted bulbous plants are grateful for some extra protection from the cold.

Good protection is provided by a layer of dead leaves or twigs, which can be spread over the plants in late autumn. This layer will have an insulating effect and will prevent deep penetration of frost. A few conifer banches or something similar can be laid over perennials. A layer of garden compost, spread over the plants in late autumn, will protect them and, at the same time, improve the soil and provide nutrients.

The layer of winter protection should be removed in early spring when the first shoots appear. The best time to remove the covering is on a cloudy, mild day. The delicate young leaves should still be protected from bright, direct sunlight.

My tip: If sunlight is very intense, the plants can be protected by covering them with a piece of sacking, a conifer branch or twigs.

Warning: Store bulbs in a place that is inaccessible to children and pets as some bulbs are toxic (see pp. 32-59).

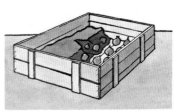

Bulbs/tubers stored correctly:
The best way to store bulbs and tubers is in a wooden box lined with a thick layer of peat, sawdust or wood shavings.

Propagation

If you want more and more spring flowers in your garden, sooner or later you will wish to try your hand at propagating your own plants. Some spring flowers are able to multiply quite happily without any help from the gardener, but others need assistance. How to propagate spring flowers is explained on the next few pages.

Propagating from seed (generative propagation)

This propagation method is not necessarily successful for all spring flowers. For many of the species covered in this volume, in particular the bulbous plants, propagation from seed is tedious and long-winded. Many varieties cannot be propagated at all in this way as they do not produce seed. Furthermore, the seedlings of many species can take from three to six years to become capable of bearing flowers.

Sowing seed is worthwhile for all biennials, particularly pansies, and some perennials, such as primulas, pasque flowers and lungwort. It is recommended that you use only pure species. Some cultivated varieties can lose their characteristic features through generative propagation, so they are best propagated by division (see p. 17).

Sowing seed: The seeds can be sown in boxes of seeding compost during the summer. In the case of dark-germinating plants, like pansies and forget-me-nots, the seed should be covered with a layer of compost (about 1 cm/¼ in thick), while the seed of light-germinating plants can be lightly pressed into the soil.

The seeds should be watered with a fine spray. Stand the seed tray in a warm, bright, but not too sunny, position and ensure even moisture but avoid wetting the soil too much. Covering the seed tray with a transparent plastic hood or PVC sheet will create a favourable atmosphere for germination.

Pricking out: As soon as the seedlings have formed two to four proper leaves, they should be pricked out. Choose strong, well-developed young plants for careful replanting in small pots or boxes containing seeding compost. Leave enough space between the plants (about 5-10 cm/2-4 in). Throw away any weak plants. After two to four weeks, you can replant them again, if you wish, to ensure that the plants flourish, although this is not absolutely necessary.

Planting out: Strongly developed young plants can be toughened up in late summer/early autumn and then planted in their final positions outside.

NB: Plants that germinate in cold conditions, like pheasant's eye, Christmas rose, winter aconite, saxifrage and bleeding heart, need the trigger of a cold temperature to germinate. Seeds of these species should be sown in the last month of autumn, placed in a cool position or even outside during the winter and then brought back into a warm place in the last month of winter.

My tip: Many bulbous plants, like snowdrops, and some perennials, like violets, form plenty of seed and look after their own propagation. While self-sowing is desirable in plants that are growing wild, it can be a nuisance in rockeries, where

2. *Remove the tiny offsets from the mature tuber and plant them, making sure they are at the correct depth.*

you will have to remove the flowerheads or seedpods before the seeds are dropped.

Vegetative propagation

Many spring flowers can be propagated in this way without any fuss. Some of the possible methods of vegetative propagation are described below.

NB: Vegetative (non-sexual) propagation means that you will obtain offspring that are identical to the mother plant as no mingling of genetic material from two parents has taken place, which is the case with generative reproduction. If you want to propagate varieties successfully in their original, typical form, you should only propagate using the vegetative method.

1. *Break off the bulbils and plant them. Check the planting depth.*

Propagation from bulbils
(Illustration 1)

Nearly all species of bulbs form tiny bulbils. Some produce many, others only a few. Narcissi, for example, produce only one or two but these are nearly as large as the original bulb. Grape hyacinths produce lots of little bulbils. Hyacinths, on the other hand, very rarely form any bulbils at all.

The bulbils are very simple to use in propagation. The mother bulb should be removed from the soil after the foliage has died back. The bulbils are then carefully broken off and planted in a propagation bed or back in the same place. Make sure they are planted at the right depth and with the right spacing (see p. 11). After one or two years, you should have plants that are capable of flowering. In some species, however, this can take up to four years – or even six years in the case of crown imperial fritillary or dog's tooth violet (*Erythronium denscanis*).

Propagation from offsets
(Illustration 2)

Tuberous plants, like ranunculus and anemones, form offsets which you can treat in the same way as described above for bulbils. You can expect plants capable of flowering after two to four years.

Propagation from divided tubers
(Illustration 3)

Species such as *Eranthis* (winter aconite) and *Ranunculae* can be propagated quite easily by dividing the tuber. Choose only larger tubers for propagation and proceed as follows. Lift the tuber from the soil after the foliage has died right down and cut it into several pieces with a clean knife, making sure that each portion still has at least one bud from which a shoot will grow. The cut surface should be dipped in

3. Cut the tuber into several pieces which should all have one or more shoot tips. Plant the pieces with the shoot tips pointing upwards.

charcoal powder (obtainable in the gardening trade) to protect it against decay or fungal infection. Then, plant the pieces with the shoot tips uppermost.

Propagating shrubs by division
(Illustration 4)

The simplest method of vegetative propagation is division. It is possible for many perennials, such as marsh marigold, blue-eyed Mary (*Omphalodes verna*), aubrieta and dwarf phlox.

Remove the plant from the soil after flowering and either break it up by hand or split it with a knife or hand trowel into fist-sized pieces. Each part should still have a few buds that are able to shoot. The parts must be planted in accordance with the requirements of the species (see pp. 32-59).

Propagation from cuttings

Some cushion-forming perennials can be propagated from cuttings, for example, *Alyssum, Arabis, Iberis* and bleeding heart (*Dicentra spectabilis*). Cuttings can be taken from the parent plant in the spring or early summer.

Taking cuttings: Using a sharp knife, cut off finger-long pieces of shoot, with four to six leaves, immediately above a bud or node in the stalk.

Rooting in water: Stand the cutting in a glass of water. When roots have formed, plant it in a seeding tray or a small pot filled with seeding compost.

Rooting in compost: Plant several cuttings in a pot or small tray filled with seeding compost. Stand them in a bright, warm position and cover the pot or tray with plastic sheeting to ensure high humidity. Once roots have formed, slowly toughen up the plant (remove the plastic cover for longer and longer periods) and, eventually, plant the cuttings outside.

My tip: If you dip the cut surface of the cuttings in rooting powder (obtainable in the gardening trade), they will form roots much faster.

4. Remove the plant from the soil to divide it.

Garden crocus with golden "powder puffs" set in delicate flower cups.

Spring flowers indoors

Tazetta narcissi, hyacinths and other bulbous plants can be used to bring a scent of spring into the house as early as Christmas. Light and warmth will awaken these plants early from their winter sleep.

Method: You will need a wide, shallow bowl and a mixture of sand, gravel and bulb compost (mixed in equal parts).

● Fill the bowl with the compost mixture and set the bulbs on top, merely pushing them down very gently but using very little pressure.

● Soak the compost with water so that the bottom of the bulb is immersed in water.

● Stand the bowl in a cool, dark place.

● Make sure there is sufficient water as the growing roots should always be in water.

● When the first shoots start appearing, gradually move the bowl into a brighter position, so that the plants can slowly become accustomed to the light and increasing warmth, until they rapidly produce flowers in bright sunlight.

NB: Hyacinths can also be brought on early in special hyacinth jars (obtainable in the gardening trade).

My tip: In addition to Tazetta narcissi, hyacinths and garden crocuses, many varieties of single and double early tulips, Kaufmann and Fosteri tulips, *Iris reticulata* and winter aconite are all quite suitable for bringing on early.

Pests and diseases

Healthy plants develop immunity

Viridiflora tulip.

Unfortunately, the warmth of the spring sun not only coaxes flowers into growth but also encourages pests and diseases. Observe your plants during the growth period and also check stored bulbs and tubers so that you can step in with preventive measures before infestation occurs.

Promoting natural immunity
The more you meet the needs of your plants with respect to choice of position, the more immunity they will develop towards pests and diseases. Weakened plants which grow feebly in the wrong position are the ideal prey for pests. The better that the plants' requirements for correct light, soil and nutrients are met, the more easily they will resist parasites and diseases. The best preventive measure is to take a good look at all possible positions and plant the right spring plants in the right places (see position, p. 8). In spite of such preventive measures, however, you will occasionally be confronted with aphids, grey mould, mice or even diseases caused by viruses or bacteria but do not be put off by these possibilities. If you act quickly enough, you will be able to put matters right and continue to enjoy your spring flowers.
My tip: Take a frequent look at your plants so that you will note any changes or abnormalities and get to the bottom of the problem. The sooner you recognize trouble, the better your chance of success in getting rid of it.

Common problems of bulbous plants
Unfortunately, most of the pests and diseases that attack bulbous plants are so stubborn that they can only be defeated by tough measures, i.e. chemical plant protection agents.
Remedy: In the most severe cases, such as an infestation with narcissus fly or a virus that is causing the deformation of parts of the plant (see. p. 21), the best and simplest action to take is to destroy the infested plants immediately. This is really the only way to avoid any further spread of the problem. As bulbous plants are generally not expensive to buy, replacing the lost bulbs is often cheaper than spending money on elaborate forms of plant protection.

My tip: Infested plants should never be thrown on the compost heap, as pests and disease-inducing microorganisms can often flourish there. Instead, throw them in the dustbin or on to a bonfire.

Plant protection agents
The use of toxic sprays to combat diseases and pests is no longer recommended. Indeed, in some countries in Europe, local district authorities have prohibited the use of such insecticides and herbicides. If the use of plant protection agents is unavoidable (e.g. in the case of bacterial decay or nematode infestation), extreme caution is advised. Make absolutely sure you read the instructions for use throroughly and then follow them meticulously as these substances damage our environment more than they benefit it.
Biological protection agents, which are less harmful to the environment, are always preferable. There are a number of gentle, natural methods to combat pests and diseases. Some of them are described in the following paragraphs. If you want more information on natural, organic gardening, you should make enquiries at your local garden centre or seek out gardening publications that promote organic methods.
Warning: Store all plant protection agents, even biological ones, in a place that is inaccessible to children and pets!

Animal pests
Quite a few animals that we normally like and enjoy watching fall under this heading. On the one hand, there are several animal "vandals" who will spoil the beauty of your flowers.
On the other hand, however, such creatures cannot be exterminated from their rightful place in the natural order. It is, therefore, best to employ

19

gentle, but effective, methods to discourage these animal pests. Here are a few tips.

Mice, voles and rabbits
These nimble, elusive rodents view your flower bulbs and tubers as scrumptious delicacies and will often inflict great damage on plants. They are very hard to combat or chase away.
Counter-measure: Protect your plants by:
● Planting bulbs and tubers in planting baskets made of plastic or wire netting (obtainable in garden centres etc.) This makes them practically inaccessible to rodents.
● Plant crown imperial fritillaries. These are considered by voles to be very nasty on account of their unpleasant smell, so these particular rodents will stay well away.

Blackbirds and sparrows
These birds in particular will go to great lengths to gobble up whole groups of crocuses, leaving behind sad, tattered petals.
Counter-measure: Attach aluminium strips to sticks pushed into the ground or set up scarecrows. This should frighten the birds away without harming them.

Slugs and snails
The young, delicate leaves of narcissi, tulips and many perennials are a favourite meal of slugs, which, particularly in a mild spring, can suddenly appear in hordes overnight.
Counter-measure: there seems to be no natural remedy against this arch-pest. The only way to limit the damage they create is by:
● setting up beer traps or snail fences (obtainable in the gardening trade);
● spraying with a brew made from fern (*Pteridium aquilinum*) (see below);
● surrounding the plants with dry

bran or shavings, which slugs dislike crawling across.

Thrips and nematodes
Thrips, namatodes and narcissus flies are tiny, inconspicuous pests. Thrips, which look like minute transparent blisters on foliage and petals, suck the sap of the plants. Affected plants generally fade and die. There are no cures for infestation by nematodes and narcissus fly (see illustration, p. 21).
Counter-measure: Only preventive measures can bring any relief. The reproductive cycle of these pests,

which overwinter in the soil, can be disturbed through intensive working of the soil. This involves carefully loosening the soil every few weeks and crumbling it up with a hand rake or something similar, working in compost to obtain a high content of humus and avoiding overfertilizing.

Fungal diseases
Microscopic fungi cause great damage to spring flowers every year. Grey mould, root and stem decay, dry rot, wet rot, rust and leaf burn are only a few members of the huge range of fungal diseases.

Biological sprays
You can obtain the dried ingredients for these sprays in the specialist garden trade, or from herbal suppliers or some chemists.

To combat mildew
Mare's tail brew (Hippuris vulgaris): Take 500 g (18 oz) fresh or 75 g (2½ oz) dried mare's tail.
● Soak the dried herb in 5 litres (9 pt) of water for about 24 hours, then bring it to the boil and let it simmer for about half an hour.
● Allow the brew to cool, strain it and dilute it with water in 1 part brew to 5 parts water.
● Spray the whole plant with the brew and then also water it with the same.

Garlic tea (when infested): You will need 25 g garlic cloves to 5 litres (9 pt) of water.
● Crush the cloves and pour on 1 litre (1¾ pt) of boiling water.
● Strain the tea and allow it to cool.
● Do not dilute. Spray the whole plant with the tea.

To combat slugs and snails (as a preventive measure or when infested)
Fermented fern brew (Pteridium aquilinum): You will need 500 g (18 oz) fresh or 50 g (1½ oz) dried fern to 5 litres (9 pt) of water.
● Stir well, allow to stand and stir daily.
● After five to seven days, when fermentation begins (small bubbles will begin to rise), strain, dilute as 1 part brew to 10 parts water and use immediately.
● Spray or water with a fine spray (both plants and soil).

To combat aphids and for a general strengthening of the plants' immunity to disease
(as a preventive measure or when infested)
Stinging nettle brew: You will need 500 g (18 oz) fresh, non-flowering plants or 100 g (3½ oz) dried leaves to 5 litres (9 pt) of water.
● Allow it to soak for 24 hours, boiling it once.
● When it has cooled, dilute it as 1 part brew to 4 parts water and spray the whole plant with the liquid.

Counter-measures: There are few remedies for fungal infections. If bulbs or other plants are infected, you should avoid planting other members of the same species in the same soil for several years as the spores of the fungi will remain viable for a long time.

Grey mould occurs fairly frequently on bulbous flowers. Various species of grey mould have a fondness for particular plants and will produce characteristic signs of damage on the plants. In tulips, one form of typical damage is called tulip fire; in narcissi, one may often find narcissus fire (see illustration, right).

Mildew appears most often on perennials and biennials, for example, primulas, wallflowers and Christmas roses. A flour-like dusting on the leaves and flowers is an unmistakable sign of infestation. To prevent this from spreading, do not site the plants too close together, make sure the soil is loose and water permeable and water in good time when conditions are very dry.

● Cut off infested shoots and leaves and spray the plant with mare's tail brew or garlic tea.

Common diseases of bulbous and tuberous plants

Grey mould (Botrytis): brown stalk and surfaces of leaves, grey mould patches, the leaves are small and often tattered, the flowers look deformed. Occurs in tulips (tulip fire), snowdrops, hyacinths, narcissi (narcissus fire) and scilla. Cut out infested parts and destroy any infested bulbs.

Basal rot: mould infestation occurs in stored bulbs. Light brown, depressed patches, the bulb decays and the inside displays a chocolate-brown discoloration. Occurs in narcissi and tulips. Infested bulbs should be destroyed immediately and the site where they were planted should not be used again for bulbous plants for several years.

Nematodes: deformed growth, yellowish lumps in the leaves, no flowers. Brown rings in the bulbs. Occurs in narcissi, tulips, snowdrops, hyacinths and bulbous irises. Infested bulbs should be destroyed immediately and infested areas should not be used again for planting bulbous plants for at least two years.

Narcissus fly: the shoots are weak, curly and grass-like or there are no shoots at all. Fat, dirty-white grubs bore holes in the bulb and the bulb begins to decay from the bottom up. Occurs in narcissi, less often in tulips and hyacinths. Destroy soft bulbs in the autumn and eaten bulbs in the spring.

Virosis: malformation of the stems, leaves, flowers; patchy, mosaic-like patterns along the veins of the leaves. Occurs in almost all bulbous plants (symptoms vary). Destroy any infested plants immediately. Avoid infestation with aphids as they are carriers of the virus.

Viral and bacterial diseases

Diseases caused by bacteria and viruses are every gardener's nightmare.

Bacteria cause a wettish, decaying rootstock and various diseases. Viral infections can be identified by deformed growth and mosaic-like patterns (see illustration, p. 21).

Counter-measures: Diseases caused by bacteria or viruses are incurable. The infested plants should be destroyed as quickly as possible.

NB: Some of the more unusual types of tulip varieties, like Rembrandt or Chamaeleon tulips, were created thanks to viral attack. These plants, which have flame-patterned, striped or veined flower petals in contrasting colours, carry a virus that causes these extraordinary colour displays. It is not known how these varieties manage to survive this viral attack. Once infected, other tulip varieties generally die.

My tip: Rembrandt or Chamaeleon tulips should be kept well isolated from any other tulips to prevent cross-infection.

King cups (marsh marigolds) are ideal plants for the moist edge of a pond. Their reflections in the water makes them look twice as abundant. Trumpet daffodils and Poeticus narcissi grow from the bank right into the meadow.

Splendour on your balcony

Garden tulip.

There is no reason why the balcony should remain bare in spring while your garden is filled with beautiful displays of flowers. Many spring plants flourish in balcony boxes, flowering profusely and bringing all the beauty of spring right up to your door.

The season for balcony flowers does not really begin until the last month of spring, after the last cold snap of the season. Before then, the worst of the winter weather can do great damage to balcony flowers. On the other hand, the flowering season on your balcony can be extended by about three months if you plant some of the less cold-sensitive spring flowers. Spring on your balcony can be just as versatile and colourful as spring in the garden. In addition to biennials like pansies, daisies and forget-me-nots, many species and varieties of bulbous and tuberous plants and small perennials can be planted in tubs. If you choose the right species and varieties and note their requirements for care, these charming plants will grace your balcony right through until it is time to plant summer flowers.

Tips on choosing plants

Many spring flowers grow perfectly well in the limited space of flower-boxes.

Choosing the right plants

Choose only small plants, such as low-growing wild species and varieties that will grow to a height of about 30 cm (12 in). Flowers that grow very tall will not have enough support and will tend to fall over in the slightest breeze (see pp. 32-59). Depending on the variety, plants of the same genus may grow to quite different sizes. *Among the tulips and narcissi*, the tall-growing varieties can be knee-high. The long, slender stems of Darwin tulips and trumpet narcissi, as well as the heavy flowers of peony tulips, are unsuitable for balcony conditions. Their rather grand-looking flowerheads look out of place on a balcony anyway. *In the case of wallflowers, anemones and narcissi*, you should also think about their final height when choosing species. Some wallflower varieties, in partic-ular those intended for use as cut flowers, may attain heights of around 70 cm (28 in) and are, therefore, totally unsuited to bal-cony positions.

NB: Make sure you pick the right varieties when you are buying seeds and bulbs! Read the information on the packet or ask a sales assistant for advice. If you still wish to plant flowers that grow tall, you will have to give them some form of support, especially in windy positions (see p. 26).

How long will flowers last in a spring tub?

There seems to be a general opin-ion that planting spring-flowering tubs is hardly worth the effort because spring flowers often bloom for such a short time. The result of this is that many a gardener fore-goes much of the pleasure to be derived from spring flowers. In actu-al fact, the flowering period of a bal-cony tub can last all spring. The trick is to choose species and vari-eties that flower both simultaneous-ly and in sequence.

For example, several varieties of tulip flower one after the other from the first to the last month of spring. The Kaufmann or water lily tulips (*Tulipa kaufmanniana*) flower very early, so you can follow them with single early tulips and end up with cottage tulips. If you plant double daisies between them, there will be no break at all in the flowering sequence. The planting example on page 29 demonstrates an uninter-rupted flowering sequence in a tub from early until late spring.

A balcony box containing late tulips, forget-me-nots, red and yellow wallflowers and daisies.

Spacing of plants

Plants require a certain amount of room to thrive. With the limited space available in a tub or large container, the number of plants you choose will have to be carefully worked out.

In ordinary balcony boxes (obtainable in garden centres etc.), which are approximately 20 cm (8 in) deep and 15 cm (6 in) wide, you should plant only really small plants. The space will fill up quickly with very few plants. If you plant them too close together, the roots will compete for growing space and the plants will not be able to develop properly.

A general rule for planting in balcony boxes is to leave a space of two to three fingers' width between the larger bulbs, although smaller bulbs can be set closer together. Leave about a hand's width of space between perennials.

You will have much more room at your disposal with *large tubs or containers* that are permanently fixed features. As they are much deeper and wider, they can accom-modate more plants (even taller ones). Tall tulips can thus be plant-ed in wind-sheltered positions with-out falling over at the first gust. Even spring-flowering shrubs, such as rhododendron varieties, and ornamental cherry trees can be planted in these large containers.

Balcony gardening

Much work is required before you can sit back and enjoy a display of colourful spring flowers on your balcony. Caring for these plants is not difficult, however, and the end result is worth all the time and effort.

Preparing the plant containers
Whether you decide to plant in the autumn or spring and whether you choose bulbs, tubers or perennials, the following rules apply.
Compost: The most suitable compost is good quality potting compost which will not form lumps or become heavy but remain water-permeable. Many different brands are obtainable in the gardening trade. Good potting compost will contain a basic reserve of nutrients which should last for the entire period of growth of your spring flowers. You can also make your own compost using garden soil (or well-sieved, clean, used soil from summer plants), bark humus and potting compost mixed in equal parts.

Add a few handfuls of coarse river sand.
Suitable containers: roomy boxes (at least 15 cm/6 in wide and 20 cm/8 in deep), large containers or large bowls. It does not matter much what material they are made of but drainage holes are essential

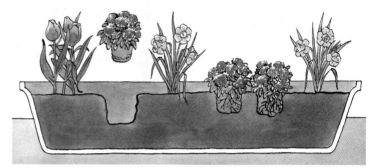

2. In spring, fill any gaps between the bulbous flowers with small herbaceous plants like daisies or pansies.

so that any surplus water can run away. Clean any used boxes thoroughly before starting.

Drainage: Spread an approximately 5-cm (2 in) thick layer of Hortag or

gravel in the bottom of the pot. Place a layer of interfacing fabric over this (obtainable in garden centres etc.). This will prevent soil being washed into the drainage layer when watering.

Autumn planting of bulbs and tubers
(Illustration 1)
Bulbs and tubers should be planted from the end of the first month of autumn until the end of the the second month of autumn at the latest.
Depth of planting: The bulbs of species that are suitable for growing on balconies are naturally quite small. They can be planted 5-8 cm (2-3 in) deep. Larger bulbs, for example those of tulips, should be planted about 10-15 cm (4-6 in) deep in the soil. It is possible to plant them at a more shallow depth in boxes than in a garden bed.
Method
● Lay a drainage layer in the pot or box and cover it with interfacing fabric.
● Fill the container with compost to a depth of about 5 cm (2 in).
● Place the larger bulbs on the compost.

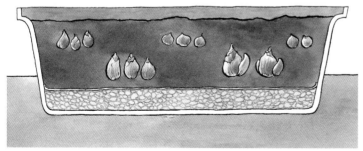

1. Bulbs in a box: The bulbs have been planted at the right depth in a small box containing a drainage layer and compost.

- Fill the container with more soil until you have reached the depth needed for the smaller bulbs and tubers. Place them on the compost and fill up the container to about 2 cm (¾ in) from the edge.
- Press the soil down lightly and water thoroughly so that the soil is moist but not wet.

NB: If you plant bulbs in autumn, they will overwinter in the box and should be protected from frost (see overwintering in balcony boxes, p. 30).

Planting perennials in autumn
Perennials can be planted at the same time as bulbs and tubers in autumn.

3. Tall, bushy plants can be supported by two sticks driven crossways into the soil.

- Place a drainage layer in the container and cover it with interfacing fabric. Pour in soil to about a hand's width deep.
- Set the plants on the layer and add more soil. The plants should sit just as deep as they did in their last pot. Press the soil down well around the roots.
- Add the bulbs and tubers. Make holes in the soil with the handle of a trowel or a dibber. Pop the bulbs/tubers into the holes and fill them with soil. Water well.

Planting in spring
Bulbs and tubers that are sprouting can be planted in the first month of spring. The same goes for perennials and biennials. Planting is best done on a mild, cloudy day so that the plants are not subjected to extreme cold or intense sunlight.
- Boxes that contain a layer of drainage material are filled 10 cm (4 in) deep with soil.
- Carefully remove the plants from their pots.
- Place the plants about 5-10 cm (2-4 in) apart and fill the rest of the container with soil. Press it down round the roots and water thoroughly.

Further spring planting
(Illustration 2)
If you only planted bulbs and tubers in the autumn, you can create more luxuriant growth in your balcony tub the following spring by planting biennials between the other plants.
- Carefully dig holes in the soil between the bulbous plants.
- Remove the plants from their pots and plant them in the holes, fill them with soil and press it down.
- Water well.

Care in the spring
The first leaves and buds will start appearing when the days get longer and the weather milder.
Watering: The flowers will need plenty of moisture to develop properly. The soil should always be moist but not wet. You can check this by pushing a finger into the soil.

4. Tulips or other long-stemmed flowers should be supported so that they do not fall over.

You only need to water if the soil feels dry at a depth of about 3.75 cm (1½ in).
Protect the plants from frost: A light frost (to about -5° C/23° F) will not harm your plants very much but the lower that temperatures drop, the more protection they will need. Hoods made of transparent plastic (bubble pack or gardeners' PVC) or folded "hats" made of newspaper can be placed over the plants to keep them a few degrees warmer.
Protect them from the weight of snow: A thin layer of snow will not harm the plants but heavy showers of sleet or slush can cause the stalks to snap. Again, use protective hoods.

Support tall plants
(Illustrations 3 and 4)
- In the case of flowers with very long stalks, push thin sticks into the soil and tie the stems to them with raffia.

Planting times in autumn and spring

Bulbous and tuberous plants can be planted either in autumn (bulbs or tubers) or in spring (as shooting plants). Perennials can be planted in the autumn but must then be well protected from frost (see overwintering, p. 30).

Planting in spring is generally safer. *Planting in autumn* is cheaper but involves more work as the boxes have to be overwintered. The advantage of planting in the autumn is that you have a greater choice of species and varieties because lots of bulbs are on sale, whereas the supply of shooting plants is not always very large in spring.

NB: Make sure you choose good quality bulbs and tubers (see p. 10). *Planting shooting bulbous and tuberous plants in spring* is simpler but more expensive. At that time (during the first and second months of spring) you can also plant smaller perennials (container plants) and biennials, for example, pansies and forget-me-nots.

NB: Buy plants with clearly visible buds that have not yet begun to shoot. At this stage of growth, the plants can cope very well with transplanting and will flower for a long time.

Choosing colours for your balcony

The following examples suggest various plants to use for creating attractive combinations of colour. The possibilities are limitless!

Yellow, red and blue: This simple trio of colours has a cheerful effect and is eye-catching.
● Suitable plants: yellow cyclamineus narcissi "Peeping Tom" and yellow ranunculus. Red Kaufmann tulips "Scarlett Eleganz". Blue forget-me-not "Amethyst". This grouping includes large, dominant flowers which blend perfectly with the tiny blue flowers of the forget-me-nots. The tulips will produce long-lasting blooms and create bold splashes of colour.

Blue, yellow and white: bright, cool spring colours.
● Suitable plants: blue grape hyacinths (*Muscari armeniacum*) "Blue Spike" and pansies (*Viola* x *wittrockiana* hybrids). Golden crocus (*Crocus ancyrensis*) and yellow double narcissi "Van Sion". White double early tulips "Schoonoord". The first to bloom are the glowing golden crocuses, followed by the tassle-like flowers of the narcissi. The pansies provide a blue carpet right from the beginning until the end of the flowering period and the finale is supplied by the shining white double tulips.

Pink, blue and white: This is a very elegant colour combination which works even for very simple plantings.
● Suitable plants: pink double early tulips "Peach Blossom". Blue forget-me-not "Compindi". White cushion-forming primula. This box will flower for weeks on end. Set off by the white of the cushion primulas, the pink tulips harmonize beautifully with the intense sky-blue of the forget-me-nots.

Pastel shades: The main role is played by soft, delicate colours.
● Suitable plants: globe primulas (*Primula denticulata*) "Grandiflora" in a light shade of violet. Yellow cowslips (*Primula veris*). Light blue glory of the snow (*Chionodoxa luciliae*). Violet (*Viola cornuta*) "Bambini mixture" in various pastel colours. Harmonizing shades of the same colours give the planting a charm that is further enhanced by the delicate flowers. The cheerful little faces of the miniature violets peek out among the primulas and bloom tirelessly until it is time for summer planting.

Shades of blue: Blue gives an optical illusion of depth and shimmers in cool, fresh hues. Blue flowers in different shades and shapes can be delightful and subtle.
● Suitable plants: forget-me-nots; hyacinths "Delfts Blauw" and "Bismarck"; cushion-forming primulas; *Scilla siberica* "Spring Beauty".

White and red: This combination works because of the contrast created between the strong shades of red and shining white.
● Suitable plants: cushion primulas in shades of red and white. Red *Tulipa praestans* "Fuselier". Red hyacinth "L'Innocence".

The small tulips produce several blooms, while the primulas form thick cushions at their feet. The "baroque" hearts of the hyacinths complete the picture. The box will remain in full bloom for several weeks.

Flowers on the balcony all spring long

This planting plan was designed for a box 1 m (40 in) long, 15 cm (6 in) wide and 20 cm (8 in) deep, and shows just how colourful and long-lasting spring can be on a balcony. Various species form eye-catching features one after another, framed by masses of blossom. The early tulips bloom in the first month of spring, producing brilliant red flowers. They are accompanied by the small, pretty cyclamineus narcissi, which bear two to three graceful blooms per stalk. By the time the first flowers have faded, the next buds are already appearing amid the foliage. Little spires of grape hyacinths create magical points of blue light; the yellow tufts of double early tulips draw the eye, while the delicate blooms of the jonquils spread their sweet scent in the last month of spring. From the beginning to the end of spring, the cushion primulas and pansies provide a constantly flowering ground cover.

List of species and varieties	Flowering time (Figures 1-4 = number of weeks)											
	1st month of spring				2nd month of spring				3rd month of spring			
	1	2	3	4	1	2	3	4	1	2	3	4
5 water lily tulips, *Tulipa kaufmanniana* "Showwinner" (glowing scarlet red)			▓	▓	▓	▓						
3 double early tulips "Monte Carlo" (glowing yellow)								▓	▓	▓		
7 cyclamineus narcissi, *Narcissus cyclamineus* "Tête à Tête" (golden yellow)	▓	▓	▓	▓	▓	▓	▓					
5 jonquils, *Narcissus jonquilla* "Baby Moon" (golden orange yellow)								▓	▓	▓	▓	▓
2 cushion primulas, *Primula vulgaris* hybrids (white)	▓	▓	▓	▓	▓	▓	▓	▓	▓	▓	▓	▓
5 grape hyacinths, *Muscari armeniacum* "Heavenly Blue" (sky blue)	▓	▓	▓	▓	▓	▓	▓	▓	▓	▓	▓	▓
2 pansies, *Viola* x *wittrockiana* hybrids "Crystal Bowl Blau" (blue) or other blue varieties			▓	▓	▓	▓	▓	▓	▓	▓	▓	▓

Care after flowering

After the last cold spell of late spring, when it is time to plant your balcony boxes for summer, you will have to remove the remains of the spring flowers.

Bulbs and tubers cannot be left in the tubs for several years as they will be unable to store enough energy to go on flowering in a box. If you have a garden, remove the plants from the box, lay them in bunches, together with any remains of leaves, in a shady place and cover them with compost. When the foliage has turned completely yellow, clean off the bulbs and tubers and store them (see temporary storage of bulbs and tubers, p. 15). In the autumn, they can be planted out in the garden. Particularly well-developed large bulbs and tubers can be reused for balcony boxes. If you have no garden, you can heel in the bulbs and tubers in a shallow box with some of the soil from the planting box and allow them to ripen in a shady place on the balcony (if the sun is strong, cover the bulbs with twigs). When the leaves have turned completely yellow (see

p. 15) store the bulbs. The healthiest-looking bulbs and tubers can be replanted in the autumn (fill up gaps with new plants). If this is inconvenient for you, give the plants to a garden owner or throw them out. After flowering, **perennials** can remain in the box if it is large enough and there will still be enough space for summer flowers, or else they can be moved to suitable positions in the garden. If you have no garden, perennials can be transplanted into another tub to continue growing on the balcony until they are required again in the spring. Otherwise, they will have to be thrown away.

My tip: The old soil/compost can be used for soil improvement in the garden (remove large roots, sprinkle the compost on to the beds and rake it in lightly). If you mix the used compost in a ratio of 2:1 with seasoned, ripe garden compost, you can use it again in a balcony box for summer plants.

Overwintering balcony boxes

The cold and frost are much more harmful to balcony plants than to flowers in the garden. If you wish to see a splendid show of blooms each spring, it is essential that bulbs and tubers grown on a balcony are well protected during the winter. For this reason the boxes should be prepared well before the first frosts of winter.

Overwintering in the garden

If you have a garden, you can place the planted boxes of bulbs and tubers in a sheltered place outside for the winter. To protect them from freezing right through, the boxes should be sunk into the soil by about two thirds or surrounded by thick bundles of twigs or conifer branches.

Overwintering indoors

The boxes can also be overwintered in the house in a position that is cool and frost-free. Light is not necessary. An unheated stairwell or a cool cellar is suitable for overwintering.

Overwintering on the balcony

(Illustration bottom left)
If you have no other facilities, you will have to prepare the boxes in situ on the balcony. The plants can cope with temperatures several degrees below freezing but if there are long periods of freezing weather, there is a danger of the soil in the boxes freezing right through, which would kill the plants.
Frost protection is absolutely essential on **unprotected balconies**. An "over-box" will probably prove to be the best solution.

● The box should be 5-10 cm (2-4 in) larger than the planting box and can be made out of wood, polystyrene sheets or strong cardboard.
● Stand the balcony box in the "over box" and fill the gaps with wood shavings, paper or other insulating material.
● Cover the box with a thick layer of conifer branches. The plants will survive fairly cold winters if they are protected in this way.

If the balcony is sheltered or you live in a region with mild winters, it will be sufficient to wrap the box in a thick layer of newspaper, wood shavings, strips of fabric or old tights, tied up in string and encased in bundles of conifer branches or twigs.

Winter protection for a balcony box: A box made of wood or polystyrene and a thick layer of wood shavings or dead leaves will protect the bulbs from freezing temperatures.

A terracotta container with wild tulips, cyclamineus narcissi, crocuses and scilla.

Stand the boxes on the floor and then slide a small plank or small pieces of timber underneath it to lift the box off the cold floor. As soon as the days become milder, you can remove the coverings and layers of insulation.

My tip: If the container is very large, you can provide winter protection, even before planting, by lining the inside of the container with poly-styrene sheets or bubble pack (leave the drainage holes free).

Watering in winter

After planting, the box should be watered once thoroughly but the soil should not be left soaking wet. This moisture will generally be suffi-cient for the next few weeks if the boxes are not placed in a position that is too warm. Mild weather will bring the bulbs to life, however, and growth will often begin as early as late winter. The sprouting bulbs will require moisture, so you may have to provide water so that the soil is just damp, even though it is still only late winter. Further watering

will only become necessary when the soil has dried out again. For boxes that are overwintered indoors, dryness of the soil will have to be checked for more regularly. The soil should always feel slightly moist, never wet. Whenever it becomes completely dry, gently add a little more water.

Flowering magic in spring

From elegant beauties in dazzling colour to humble little gems – the range of spring flowers is enormous. The following pages will introduce you to a selection of enchanting spring flowers and give useful notes on their care.

Poeticus narcissi.

These short descriptions of the plants, together with the accompanying photographs and helpful tips on their care, should make it easier for you to choose suitable plants for your garden and balcony from the wide range of most commonly available and popular spring flowers, including tulips, narcissi, hyacinths, snowdrops and both sun-loving and shade-loving perennial and biennial herbaceous plants. In addition to the many plants featured here there are, of course, many more flowers that bloom during the months of spring but lack of space makes it impossible to mention all of them. The varieties mentioned here are merely representative of the great number of further extremely interesting varieties in some groups and species.

Glossary of keywords

The botanical name: gives an exact description of the plant (see p. 7).
Family: gives the taxonomy of the plant.
Flowering time and height: refer to the plant being described and may vary according to the variety. Please ask your supplier about any other particular variety.
Warning: supplies information on the toxicity of a plant or states whether it may cause a skin irritation.
Requirements: information on the optimal requirements (light, warmth, moisture, soil).
Care: details important measures of care.
Planting: here you will find ideal planting times, depths and spacing.
Use: the positions where the plant will do particularly well and look effective.

Elegant colours in the garden: Towards the end of spring, parrot tulips are still in full bloom as the first summer flowers, such as bearded iris, begin to open. Lacy forget-me-nots close the gaps between tall-growing perennials.

An interesting contrast is created by combining single early tulips with candytuft as an underplanting.

Tulips

Tulips lend colour to the spring garden. From elegant white to rich red, the countless species and varieties display a wealth of colours and beautiful flowers.

Botanical name: Tulipa.
Family: Liliaceae.
Flowering time: mid-spring to early summer.
NB: according to international classification, tulips are divided into four groups containing a total of fifteen divisions.
Warning: tulip bulbs are toxic and may irritate the skin!

Early tulips
Flowering time: from the middle to the end of the second month of spring.
Height: about 20-35 cm (8-10 in).
To this group belong the single early tulips (30 cm/12 in), with flowers that are often scented; also the double early varieties, a shorter-stemmed group with voluptuous flowers.

Lily-flowered tulip.

Viridiflora tulip.

Greigii tulips with decorative leaf patterns.

Medium early tulips
Flowering times: mid- to late spring.
Height: about 35-50 cm (14-20 in).
These medium early flowering tulips comprise the Mendel tulips, robust varieties which can cope with long periods of rain without coming to any harm, and the often two-coloured Triumph tulips, which are also weather-hardy. Also included in this group are the Darwin hybrid tulips, the largest, most splendid varieties of all garden tulips; their flowers grow on firm, knee-high stalks and offer brilliant colours.

Late tulips
(Photographs above and below left)
Flowering times: late spring to early summer.

Height: 40-70 cm (16-28 in).
The Lily tulips, Darwin tulips and Parrot tulips all belong to this group. Cottage tulips are often the very latest flowering tulips of all and are prized for their soft shades. Viridiflora tulips are also counted among this group. Double late tulips resemble peonies in appearance but are sensitive to wind and rain. Rembrandt tulips display an exotic range of colours.

Wild species
(Photograph above right)
Flowering time: mid- to late spring.
Height: 10-40 cm (4-16 in).
The fourth group comprises all wild species and their hybrids, also called "botanical tulips". Among them are the *kauffmanniana* tulips, also called water lily tulips because of the shape of their flowers. *Fosteriana* tulips have the largest blooms of all tulips. *Greigii* tulips also have attractively coloured foliage. Among them are a number of attractive species, such as the dwarfs, for example, the luxuriant

yellow-flowering *Tulipa tarda*, as well as tall-growing species, like the Weinberg tulip (*Tulipa sylvestris*).

Tips on the care of tulips
Requirements: sunny to slightly shady, neutral to slightly alkaline sandy or loamy soil. Cannot stand acid or overfertilized soil.
Care: cut off faded flowers immediately. Remove garden tulips from the soil every few years and replant them in a different position. Every autumn, fertilize them with garden compost. Wild species need a dry position in summer; fertilize sparingly.
Planting: the best time is early to mid-autumn, about 5-10 cm (2-4 in) deep with a spacing of about 10-15 cm (4-6 in). Do not forget a drainage layer as protection against waterlogging (see p. 26).
Use: for specially attractive borders use garden tulips; botanical tulips for rockeries or nature gardens. Single early tulips and the wild species are well suited to balconies.

Narcissi

Easter is daffodil and narcissus time. This genus has a lot more to offer than just the ever-popular daffodil with its glowing golden trumpets. There is a truly astonishing range of varieties.

Botanical name: Narcissus.
Family: Amaryllidaceae.
Flowering time: early spring to early summer.
Warning: narcissi are toxic and the plant's sap may cause skin irritation!

The name Lent lily proves that this plant is firmly established in folklore. The classic Easter flower is the pure yellow trumpet narcissus which forms just one group of the prolific genus of *Narcissi.* There are about 10,000 varieties divided into eleven divisions, which include large and small garden narcissi as well as wild narcissi.
The basis for their classification is the shape of the flower and its origin.
The flowers of narcissi consist of outer petals arranged in a star shape and inner petals which come in varying shapes.

Large garden narcissi
(Photograph right)
Lovers of elegant flowers will much appreciate the group of large garden narcissi. The shape of the inner petals has given the two groups their names.
Daffodils (Lent lilies) have inner petals that are fused into a trumpet-shape that can be as long as the outer petals but may be even longer.
Flowering time: early to mid-spring.

Daffodils are symbols of Easter and spring.

Height: 40-50 cm (16-20 in).
Cup narcissi have bowl-shaped inner petals which are shorter than the outer petals.
Flowering time: mid- to late spring.
Height: 30-45 cm (12-18 in).
Popular varieties: "King Alfred" and "Golden Harvest" among the daffodils, and "Fortune", "Flower Record" and "Ice Follies" among the cup narcissi.
These two groups can have outer and inner petals that are yellow or white, the inner petals may even be red.

Small garden narcissi
(Photograph p. 37 top)
Enchanting flower shapes and delicate beauty are the main features of this small garden narcissus.
Double narcissi present an unusual picture as their complicated inner petals resemble those of orchids.
Flowering times: mid- to late spring.
Height: 30-50 cm (12-20 in).
Angel's tears or Triandus narcissi are graceful, delicate garden flowers. The stalk usually carries several pendulous flowers with petals that curl back.
Flowering time: mid- to late spring.
Height: 25-60 cm (10-24 in).

Cyclamen or Cyclamineus narcissi are particularly graceful harbingers of spring. They have been given this name because their petals are turned back like those of cyclamen.
Flowering time: early to mid-spring.
Height: up to 40 cm (16 in).
Jonquils or scented narcissi have several sweetly scented, delicate flowers on each stalk. Jonquils must be planted in a warm, sheltered position and require winter protection.
Flowering time: late spring to early summer.
Height: 25-50 cm (10-20 in).
Tazettas or Poetaz narcissi produce several small, pleasantly scented flowers. They are excellent for propagating (see p. 18). They will require winter protection in the garden.
Flowering time: mid- to late spring.
Height: 30-45 cm (12-18 in).
Poeticus or poet's narcissus present an incomparably beautiful sight, particularly if the white, scented flowers are allowed to unfold in long grass. The inner petals are very flat and are often edged in red.
Flowering time: late spring.
Height: up to 40 cm (16 in).

Wild narcissi
Wild narcissi are mainly delicate plants. The robust species are suitable for growing outside as well as in bowls. One of the most striking species is the hoop petticoat narcissus (*Narcissus bulbocodium*) whose yellow flowers look just like tiny ballerinas.

Other narcissi
The last group encompasses all narcissi which do not belong in any of the previously mentioned groups on account of their unusual appearance. Worth mentioning are the split-corona and the orchid-flowering narcissi.

Tazetta narcissi are charming dwarf narcissi for the rockery.

Tips on the care of narcissi
Requirements: sunny to semi-shady positions. Any normal, not too heavy, garden soil that is free of waterlogging, even acid soils.
Care: very easy to cultivate; will flower regularly every year without being replanted. Remove dead flowerheads.
Planting: in early autumn at the latest; large garden narcissi 15-20 cm (6-8 in) deep; smaller species 10 cm (4 in) deep.
Use: large narcissi for flowerbeds or in groups, at the edges of groups of trees or bushes; small wild species in rockeries or at the edge of a pond. All small varieties are suitable for the balcony.

Poeticus narcissi.

A profusion of popular varieties of garden crocus.

Crocuses

Crocuses are some of the first flowers of spring and always attract attention with their cheerful, brightly coloured flowers. A lawn covered in multi-coloured crocuses is a lovely sight.

Botanical name: Crocus.
Family: Iridaceae.
Flowering time: last month of winter to mid-spring.
Height: 6-12 cm (2¼ -4¾ in).
NB: In addition to the many spring-flowering species, the genus *Crocus* also includes some autumn-flowering species which are not covered here.

Garden crocuses
(Photograph above)
Without doubt, the most striking crocuses are the brilliantly coloured, large-flowered garden hybrids. Their large, funnel-shaped flowers appear before the long, narrow leaves and open wide in the warm spring sun. The dominant colours are white, yellow and violet, but some varieties have striped flowers. These varieties are derived from *Crocus chrysanthus* and *Crocus vernus*, proliferate

well by themselves and are also suitable for planting in a bowl. **Popular varieties** of garden crocuses are shown in the photograph on page 38: "Pickwick, "Remembrance", "Jeanne d'Arc", "Haarlem Gem", "Early Perfection", "Vanguard" and "Purpureus Grandiflorus".

Wild species
(Photographs right and below)
The wild crocuses cannot quite compete with the giant flowers of the garden crocuses but they are not far behind in growth and splendid colour. *Crocus tomasinianus* is sometimes called the "elf crocus" and is highly recommended for its long flowering time (late winter to early spring). The species has lavender blue flowers but there are also white and purple varieties. The Ankara crocus (*Crocus ancyrensis*) and the early spring crocus (*Crocus chrysanthus*) provide a display of beautiful, complementary colours in the company of *Crocus tomasinianus*.
Crocus imperati and *Crocus sieberi* bloom even earlier. In the last month of winter, the first warming rays of the sun coax their delicate flowers from the earth. The latter, in particular, is considered to be one of the most beautiful crocuses for the garden. The gold crocus (*Crocus flavus*) produces glowing golden flowers. It will proliferate well by itself. The name alone conjures up the beauty of the gold brocade or wallflower crocus (*Crocus angustifolius*). A similarly apt name is that of the silver brocade crocus (*Crocus versicolor var. picturatus*) whose white flowers display a tracery of violet-coloured veins.

Crocus tomasinianus and Crocus ancyrensis.

Tips on the care of crocuses
Requirements: they will thrive in full sun in humus-rich, well-drained soil.
Care: in summer, the small corms (bulbs) need dry soil to ripen properly and it is necessary to make sure that the soil is well drained at all times. Crocuses flower better on poor soil, so fertilizing is not necessary.
Planting: in the second month of autumn, 5-10 cm (2-4 in) deep, spaced 5-10 cm (2-4 in) apart and covered with a layer of ripe garden compost.
Use: in flowerbeds and lawns. Wild crocuses can also be planted under deciduous trees; they will not be in shade because their flowering time is so early. All species are suitable for balconies, *Crocus vernus* particularly so.
Special note: birds can be a nuisance, although they only peck at the yellow flowers. The only counter-measure is to do without yellow species and varieties. Sometimes birds can be frightened away by toy windmills on sticks

Crocus albiflorus.

placed among the crocuses.
NB: green areas (lawns etc.) covered in proliferating crocuses should not be mowed before the end of spring as it takes that long for the narrow, grass-like crocus leaves to store enough reserves to give the following year's growth the necessary strength.

Fritillaries

This name includes both the large-flowered species like *Fritillaria imperialis* and its delicate relatives, such as the snake's head fritillary (*Fritillaria meleagris*).

Crown imperial
Botanical name: Fritillaria imperialis.
Family: Liliaceae.
Flowering time: mid- to late spring.
Height: 90-120 cm (36-40 in).

The best known species, out of almost 100 species of the genus *Fritillaria*, is the crown imperial (*Fritillaria imperialis*). Glowing, coloured bells hang in a ring below a spiky head of leaves, and golden yellow stamens protrude from each bell. The regal elegance of these plants has always been popular in rustic gardens and it is one of the oldest garden plants. The fiery orange flowers have been the source of many legends. This plant was reputed to have been rebuked for its arrogance by Christ in the Garden of Gethsemane; ever since then it has hung its head and tears fall from its flowers.
Requirements: sunny position; loose, nutrient-rich soil.
Care: if necessary, fertilize when it starts shooting; cut off faded flowers and leaves.
Planting: late summer to early autumn, 20-25 cm (8-10 in) deep, slightly tilted on a bed of sand, so that no moisture can accumulate at the stem neck or at the bottom of the bulb.
Use: in borders and flowerbeds.
Special note: the bulbs give off an unpleasant smell which is effective in frightening off voles. This makes this plant very useful for controlling voles in the garden.

Crown imperial fritillary, one of the oldest garden flowers.

The original fritillary had orange-red flowers but red and yellow varieties also exist. "Rubra Maxima", "Lutea" and "Aurora" are popular for the garden. Fritillaria raddeana, which originates from Iran, is very similar but more delicate and has greenish-yellow flowers.

Fritillaria acmopetala.

Snake's head fritillary is a good name for this graceful plant.

Snake's head fritillary

Botanical name: Fritillaria meleagris.
Family: Liliaceae.
Flowering time: mid- to late spring.
Height: 20-30 cm (8-12 in).
Warning: this plant is toxic!

The snake's head fritillary is humbler than its tall cousin, at a height of only 20-30 cm (8-12 in). It has a characteristic and unusual checked pattern on its bell-shaped flowers. These plants can sometimes be found growing wild in damp meadows but you should never dig up plants in the wild as it is a protected species! This means that neither the plant nor its seed may be removed from its natural habitat. You will find a number of beautiful varieties in the gardening trade, for example, the pure white "Aphrodite", the purple green "Artemis" or the large-flowered "Poseidon" in shades of reddish-purple. Snake's head fritillaries are very easy to care for if they are planted in the right position. One thing to note is that the soil should be free of chalk or lime. They thrive particularly well in marshy ground or at the edge of water where the soil is always damp. They propagate from bulbils and, in time, large groups will form.

Requirements: a sunny to semi-shady position in moist, humus-rich, lime-free soil.
Care: fairly undemanding. The bulbs are not easy to store.
Planting: late summer/early autumn; 5-10 cm (2-4 in) deep.
Use: at the edges of groups of trees or bushes, watersides, balconies.
Special note: snake's head fritillaries are much loved by bees which will visit them to seek nectar.

Other fritillaries

Botanical name: Fritillaria species.
Family: Liliaceae.
Flowering time: early to late spring.
Height: 15-40 cm (6-16 in).

Many other attractive species can be grown in the garden, for example:

● The very undemanding *Fritillaria acmopetala* produces knee-high stems with nodding flowers in surprisingly beautiful shades of olive green and reddish-brown during mid- to late spring.

● The almost black flowers of *Fritillaria camtschatcensis*, a species which abhors lime, have a special charm of their own.

● The pale yellow flowers of the exotic *Fritillaria pallidiflora* are most attractive.

● The Persian fritillary (*Fritillaria persica*) exudes a wonderful scent from its plum-coloured flowers. It is relatively easy to cultivate but propagates very slowly.

Requirements: sunny to semi-shady position, in humus-rich soil.
Care: needs winter protection.
Planting: early autumn, 7-8 cm (2¾ -3 in) deep.
Use: rockeries; *Fritillaria pallidiflora* will also do well on balconies.

The first signs of spring

The snow may not even have quite melted and the icy hand of Jack Frost may still linger as the winter aconites, snow-drops and snowflakes open their delicate flowers.

Snowdrops
Botanical name: *Galanthus* species.
Family: *Almaryllidaceae.*
Flowering time: late winter to early spring.
Height: 5-20 cm (2-8 in).
Warning: this plant is toxic!

The snowdrop features in many old stories, for example, Eastern European peasants were once thought to dig up the bulbs as soon as the snow melted, so that witches and wizards could not put spells on the cows to make their milk dry up. This practice is not recommended as the plant is toxic but perhaps the power thus ascribed to snowdrops has something to do with the name *Galanthus*, which means "milk flower". Snowdrops were known 2,000 years ago and were hailed as messengers of spring. It is hard to believe that they are related to the majestic *Hippeastrum* as their green-edged flowers are nothing like the conspicuous flowers of that species. Snowdrops have their own special charm, however, and should be included in every garden.

● The most widespread species of snowdrop, which grows wild in some parts of Europe, is *Galanthus nivalis*. It soon produces seeds in semi-shady positions and establish-es large colonies. This species gave

The botanical name Galanthus means "milk flower".

rise to many cultivated varieties, including double types.

● *Galanthus elwesii* is much larger and stronger and sometimes pro-duces its large, striking flowers as early as the second month of winter.
Requirements: sunny to semi-shady position in humus-rich, loose soil; plenty of moisture in spring; dry in the summer. *Galanthus elwesii* likes a sunny position.
Care: do not fertilize; allow the

foliage to dry out after flowering.
Planting: first to second month of autumn; 5-8 cm (2-3 in) deep in small groups.
Use: along the edges of trees or in informal lawns.

Eranthis hyemalis (winter aconite).

Snowflakes have been planted in gardens since the fifteenth century.

Winter aconite
Botanical name: Eranthis species.
Family: Ranunculaceae.
Flowering time: late winter to early spring.
Height: 5-15 cm (2-6 in).

The winter aconite, with its golden inflorescences, opens its petals early in the last month of winter. If you plant all the different varieties together, the flowering time, which is quite short for each individual variety, can be extended to many weeks. The winter aconite (*Eranthis hyemalis*) is the first to flower in late winter; then, in early spring, it is followed by the Cilician winter aconite (*Eranthis cilicica*) and finally by *Eranthis* x *tubergenii* which can bloom right up into the second month of spring.
Requirements: sunny to semi-shady position; humus-rich, loose soil, neutral to slightly alkaline.
Care: very undemanding.
Planting: early autumn, 5-8 cm (2-3 in) deep, spaced at 5-10 cm (2-4 in); allow the tubers to soak in lukewarm water overnight before they are planted.
Use: under trees or bushes, in rockeries or lawns.

Snowflakes
Botanical name: Leucojum vernum.
Family: Amaryllidaceae.
Flowering time: early to mid-spring.
Height: about 20 cm (8 in).
Warning: this plant is toxic!

This flower strongly resembles the snowdrop in that its flowers display similar colours and markings. The natural occurrence of this plant in the wild has fallen drastically in recent years but thriving colonies can be found in gardens.
During the first and second months of spring their creamy white flowers, with their green petal tips, stand out even at a distance. The strap-like leaves are dark green and die back after flowering.
● *Leucojum vagneri*, the Hungarian snowflake, is considered to be particularly robust and striking. Usually, two flowers, with yellowish-green tips, appear on each stalk, forming a very attractive arrangement.
Requirements: semi-shady position; humus-rich, evenly moist soil.

Care: the plants should not be cut back too early so that the seeds can ripen and propagation is assured.
Planting: in early autumn, about 10 cm (4 in) deep, in small groups.
Use: edging for trees and bushes; along the banks of ponds etc.

Hyacinth beauties in shades of white and pink, blending with similar shades of primulas and daisies.

Hyacinths

The colours are beautiful, the scent is glorious and they lend a special magic to the springtime garden.

Botanical name: Hyacinthus orientalis.
Family: Liliaceae.
Flowering time: mid- to late spring.
Height: about 30 cm (12 in).
Warning: Hyacinths may cause skin irritation in some sensitive people.

The plump flowerheads of hyacinths are admired by many for their fresh colours and bewitching scent.
In the Middle Ages it was believed that merely gazing at a hyacinth could free one from all the sufferings of body and soul. In the language of flowers they represent joy and gentle love.
Whether in the garden, on a balcony or patio or grown as an indoor plant, hyacinths create an attractive picture that is hard to ignore.

Many varieties

Early varieties of hyacinths did not display the dense flowerheads we know today, as their star-shaped, individual flowers hung loosely from the stem.

Just like tulips, these flowers were once objects of financial speculation and were sold for high prices. Over the years, the great interest that developed in cultivating them gave rise to a wide range of different varieties.

The spectrum of colours extends from pure white through yellow, pink, apricot, red and orange to darkest violet and black. The varieties are not only distinguished by colour but also by their flowering time. Early varieties bloom in mid-spring, medium early ones towards the end of the second month of spring and late varieties in the last month of spring. The Multiflora hyacinths, which have been around since 1912, bloom very early. They form several inflorescences which have very few flowers. Bushy growth is obtained by cutting out the main inflorescence.

Requirements: the position should be sheltered and sunny; the soil humus-rich with plenty of nutrients. Make sure the soil is well drained.

Care: provide protection from frost with a layer of dead leaves or twigs, particularly in regions with harsh weather. The hyacinths can be left in the ground for several years in favourable positions but eventually the inflorescences will become less robust and more open. You can also dig up the bulbs after flowering and store them in a dry place until they are planted again in the autumn (see p. 15).

Planting: the larger the bulbs, the more luxuriant the flowers. Slightly smaller bulbs (about 5 cm/2 in in diameter and 15 cm/6 in in circumference) are suitable for planting outside. Plant the bulbs in early to

A colourful bowl of hyacinths, tulips, crocuses and snowdrops.

mid-autumn, about 8-15 cm (3-6 in) deep and spaced 15-20 cm (6-8 in) apart.

Use: they look best in conspicuous positions where their plump flowerheads will be in full view. Always plant groups of five or more specimens. They are also well suited to balcony boxes and bowls and look good combined with other bulbous plants.

Special note: hyacinths propagate easily. Large bulbs, with a diameter of at least 18 cm (7 in), should be used (see propagation, p. 18).

Two medium-early hyacinth varieties: pale yellow "Yellow Hammer" and blue "Concorde". The blue "Bismarck", the pure white "L'Innocence", the light pink "Anne-Marie" and the dark pink "Pink Pearl" are also very popular.

Blue spring-flowering plants

All of the following flowers are graceful in appearance and have an undemanding nature. They also compete with each other to produce the most brilliant shades of blue, like precious gems amid abundant foliage. Most species form dense colonies which carpet the ground.

Scilla and Kaufmann tulips in harmonious combination.

Tips on care
The following details apply to all of the flowers mentioned on these two pages.
Requirements: sunny to semi-shady positions; in humus-rich soil.
Care: undemanding.
Planting: first and second months of autumn; 8 cm (3 in) deep, in groups.
Use: along the edges of trees, rockeries, in the lawn, in balcony boxes and bowls.
Warning: scilla are toxic!

Scilla
(Photograph top right)
Botanical name: Scilla species.
Family: Liliaceae.
Flowering time: first and second months of spring.
Height: 5-20 cm (2-8 in).
Warning: this plant is toxic!

The most important of these species is *Scilla sibirica* which forms dense mats of clear blue, star-shaped flowers. "Spring Beauty" has the most intense shade of blue and the largest flowers. The flowers of *Scilla mischtschenkoana,* by

comparison, shine like delicate porcelain and begin to open at the same time as snowdrops and winter aconites. Pale blue, turquoise or azure are the shades of the flowers of the two-leaved *Scilla bifolia;* white and pink sports are also seen.

Grape hyacinths
(Small photograph, right)
Botanical name: Muscari species.
Family: Liliaceae.
Flowering time: early to late spring.
Height: 10-30 cm (4-12 in).

Grape hyacinths produce flowers that seem to reflect the blue of the sky. Their slender spires give any flowerbed a slightly Far Eastern flavour. Many of the 50 or so species of the genus *Muscari* are suitable for growing in the garden and all are undemanding and tough. *Muscari armeniacum,* for example, forms prolific colonies. *Muscari botryoides* blooms in the second and third months of spring and has cylindrical flowers. Lovers of seductive scents will soon come to appre-

Grape hyacinth (Muscari botryoides).

ciate *Muscari neglectum.* The feather hyacinth (*Muscari comosum* "Plumosum") will delight you with its pretty, feathery, bushy flowers.

Bluebells
(Photograph p. 47, left)
Botanical name: Endymion species.
Family: Liliaceae.
Flowering time: second to third months of spring.
Height: 20-40 cm (8-16 in).

Brodiaea laxa (syn. Triteleia laxa) is a rarity in the garden. The flowers are very elegant and are often used as cut flowers.

The Spanish bluebell (Endymion hispanicus) in a wild garden.

Chionodoxa sardensis.

The bluebell or wild hyacinth (*Endymion nonscriptus*) and the Spanish hyacinth (*Endymion hispanicus*) were once ascribed to the genus *Scilla*.

Glory of the snow
(Photograph, bottom right)
Botanical name: *Chionodoxa* species.
Family: *Liliaceae.*
Flowering time: first to second months of spring.
Height: 10-20 cm (4-8 in).

The common name of *Chionodoxa*, glory of the snow, is a most poetic description of this charming little plant which flowers early,

sometimes just as the last snows are melting. *Chionodoxa luciliae* is the most popular species for planting in the garden. The stem carries about ten shining, blue, star-shaped flowers with white centres. Some varieties are pink. *Chionodoxa gigantea* has lavender blue flowers; those of *Chionodoxa sardensis* are gentian blue.

Iris

Small and delicate best describes these iris species. Their distinctive flowers in many lovely colours make these graceful plants an extravagant treat in the garden or on a balcony.

Botanical name: Iris species.
Family: Iridaceae.
Flowering time: late winter to late spring.
Height: 10-40 cm (4-16 in).
Warning: iris bulbs are toxic!

In Ancient Greece, Iris was the golden-winged messenger of the gods and the goddess of the rainbow. She gave her name to the many-coloured plant genus *Iris*, which comprises some 200 species, with several thousand varieties. These exotic flowers are also sometimes called the "orchid of the north". Under the name fleur de lys or Bourbon lily, the iris is probably the most famous of all heraldic plants and the old flag of France bore several stylized fleurs de lys on a plain background until it was replaced by the tricolor. The flowers, consisting of three falls (hanging petals) and three standards (inner petals) form unique shapes, with their colours providing further charm. Within this large genus the spring-flowering species – in particular the bulbous ones – play a special role.

Iris bucharica forms beautiful clumps.

Gems for your rockery
(Photograph above)
Iris bucharica, which is about 40 cm (16 in) tall, has a most unusual-looking head. The scented flowers are yellow and white, appear in April and resemble stag antlers, which is why it is sometimes called the antler iris. It belongs to the group of Juno irises whose standards (inner petals) are not upright but protrude sideways. This group also includes some rarer species, for example, *Iris graeberiana*, a delicate, lavender blue plant which flowers in late spring and grows about 30 cm (12 in) tall. The Juno iris is very similar to *Iris reticulata*, one of the bulbous irises.

The bulbous irises
(Photograph p. 49, left)
The season of flowering irises begins as early as the last month of winter when the flowers appear on 10-20 cm (4-8 in) tall stems. Their blue or yellow petals flutter in the breeze (hence the name "flag") and make an eye-catching feature in the garden.
Tried and tested species and varieties
The canary yellow flowers of *Iris danfordiae* have olive green markings and a very pleasant scent. *Iris histrio* appears in the striking costume of a harlequin, which gives it its botanical name. *Iris histrioides* is not to be outdone in its equally fashionable "outfit". Depending on the variety, the flowers are light blue, dark blue or violet blue with yellow, orange or violet-black markings.

ris reticulata flowers very early.

Dwarf iris "Three Smokes".

Dwarf iris "Lady".

The shoots often push through the thawing snow and they reach their peak of flowering during the last month of winter and the first month of spring. The inconspicuous, grass-like leaves appear after the flowers are over.

ris reticulata is named for its bulb which is enveloped in a net-like sheath. This plant is easy to care for. The flowers of its many different varieties come in all shades of blue. "Harmony" is a sky-blue variety with petals sporting a shining yellow central stripe. "Katharina Hodgkin" is a hybrid with unusual colours; its delicate yellow flowers are tinged with a breath of cream and blue. *NB:* many bulbous iris species or varieties make wonderful cut flowers which will stay fresh in a vase for a very long time.

Requirements: sunny to semi-sunny position in permeable, poor, stony to loamy, slightly chalky soil. *Care:* waterlogging must be avoided (see drainage, p. 26). During the summer, the bulbs require dry soil for ripening. If the summer is wet, protect the plants from too much moisture by covering them with glass or plastic sheeting. *Planting:* the bulbs should be planted in the second month of autumn, 5-8 cm (2-3 in) deep, preferably in a sand-loam mixture.

Use: in rockeries, on the tops of drystone walls, in balcony boxes and bowls. Propagates easily. *Warning:* these plants are toxic!

Dwarf bearded iris
(Photographs, centre top and right)
Most people are familiar with the dignified little bearded iris in a summer flowerbed. In contrast to the species described above, the bearded iris does not grow from a bulb but from a rhizome, which is a thickened underground stem. Short representatives of this group only grow about 25 cm (10 in) tall and flower as early as mid- to late spring. Their flowers are brilliantly coloured and just as splendid as their tall summer relatives. There is an overwhelming range of varieties and the spectrum of colours includes almost all shades. The beards on the falls (outer, hanging petals) are often in a contrasting colour to the rest of the petals and create flowers of great visual interest.
Popular varieties: the light lemon-coloured "Lemon Puff", the bronze "Gingerbread Man", the dark violet "Cyanea", the ruby red "Little Rosy Wings" and the white and blue veined "Knick Knack".
Requirements: full sunlight, in dry, permeable, neutral to slightly alkaline soil.

Care: propagate from division of the rhizomes. Avoid waterlogging (see drainage, p. 26).
Planting: the rhizomes should be planted in shallow holes in the autumn. Dig a shallow, circular hole, place the rhizome in the slightly raised centre, carefully spread out the roots and cover with a thin layer of soil. Do not forget to provide a drainage layer!
Use: in rockeries or on a patio, in large bowls or containers between clumps of grass, cushion-forming plants and bulbous flowers.

The plump, many-coloured flowers of Ranunculus planted together in one large bowl.

Spring rarities

Alongside the ever-popular flowers like tulips and narcissi, we must not forget to mention some of the rarer beauties of spring. There is a large choice of many graceful as well as decorative species.

Ranunculae and anemones
(Photographs, above and on p. 51)
Botanical name: *Ranunuculus asiaticus* and *Anemone* species.
Family: *Ranunculaceae.*
Flowering time: late winter to late spring.
Height: 10-30 cm (4-12 in).
Warning: *Ranunculae, Anemone nemorosa* and *Anemone blanda* are toxic!
Requirements: *Ranunculae* in sunny to semi-shady positions;

Anemone species in semi-shady to shady places in fresh, humus-rich, lime-containing soil.
Planting: plant *Ranunculae* tubers in a sheltered spot in the first month of spring and allow them to shoot. Anemones can be planted in colonies in the first and second months of summer, 5-8 cm (2-3 in) deep.
Care: undemanding, provided they are planted in the right position.
Use: *Ranunculae* in flowerbeds and bowls; anemones under trees.

Anemone blanda flowers from the first to second month of spring in shades of violet, pink or white. It is self-sowing and forms vigorous colonies.

Windflowers or wood anemones (*Anemone nemorosa*) love to grow under deciduous trees and form extensive carpets of white flowers. This is the variety "Robinsoniana" with delicate lavender blue flowers.

Cyclamen, the small relatives of the popular indoor plants, are charming, hardy garden flowers that are always much admired.
Botanical name: *Cyclamen* species.
Family: *Primulaceae.*
Flowering time: first to second months of spring.
Height: 5-20 cm (2-8 in) tall.
Warning: these plants are toxic!

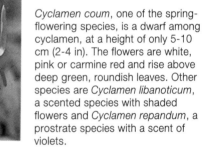

Dog's tooth violet (*Erythronium*) is a graceful plant for the garden.
Botanical name: *Erythronium* species.
Family: *Liliaceae.*
Flowering time: first to last month of spring.
Height: 10-40 cm (4-16 in).

Purple-spotted leaves and pink, gracefully curving flower bells are characteristic of the dog's tooth violet (*Erythronium dens-canis*). The flowers of *Erythronium revolutum* change colour after opening in

shades that graduate from cream to pink. The bells of *Erythronium tuolumnense* are a brilliant yellow.
Requirements: semi-shady position, in loose, fresh, slightly acidic garden soil.
Planting: the last month of spring, 10 cm (4 in) deep, spaced 10 cm (4 in) apart.
Care: fairly undemanding if positioned correctly.
Use: around the edge of trees and bushes, in rockeries.
(**The photographs:** Left, yellow "Pagoda"; right, pink "Purple King".)

Cyclamen coum, one of the spring-flowering species, is a dwarf among cyclamen, at a height of only 5-10 cm (2-4 in). The flowers are white, pink or carmine red and rise above deep green, roundish leaves. Other species are *Cyclamen libanoticum*, a scented species with shaded flowers and *Cyclamen repandum*, a prostrate species with a scent of violets.
Requirements: sunny to semi-shady position in neutral to slightly alkaline soil.
Planting: in the first month of autumn, about 5 cm (2 in) deep.
Care: undemanding if placed in the right position.
Use: along the edges of trees or bushes, in rockeries, particularly attractive in wild gardens.

Sun-loving perennials

Herbaceous perennials that like plenty of sunlight will endow your garden with a wealth of colourful flowers. Some of the most prolific flowering plants are the primulas, which come in so many colours that one has to watch out when choosing plants in case the garden becomes too colourful!

When the sun's warming rays penetrate the wintry soil, plants quickly spring to life. The golden cups of pheasant's eye (*Adonis vernalis*) open as early as the last month of winter on sunny slopes of rockeries, together with the nodding heads of the pasque flower (*Pulsatilla* species) and the golden bells of *Primula veris*. Leopard's bane (*Doronicum*), *Bergenia* and bleeding heart (*Dicentra spectabilis*) do not begin to flower until spring has well and truly arrived.

Tips on the care of sun-loving herbaceous perennials

These perennials are all easy to grow and will flower without a lot of time-consuming care. Only bleeding heart is a little more demanding and will take several years to develop into a flourishing plant.
Requirements: with few exceptions, all the species mentioned here will manage in ordinary garden soil.
Planting: see planting perennials, page 11 and planting times, page 28.
Care: always remove dead heads as soon as possible. Large colonies should be rejuvenated every few years by dividing them.

Bergenia species, family *Saxifragaceae*, flowering time first to last month of spring, are also called elephant's ear because of their large leaves. They are suitable for rockeries or a dry pond edging. Some species have vivid green leaves; others have vividly coloured foliage in the autumn. The flowers come in all shades of pink to red.

Pheasant's eye, *Adonis vernalis*, family *Ranunculaceae*, flowering time last month of winter to second month of spring, requires poor, chalky, dry soil. Suitable for dry and stony beds. *Adonis amurensis* is another pretty species with very decorative foliage.
Warning: this plant is toxic!

Leopard's bane, *Doronicum* species, family *Compositae*, flowering time from the second to third month of spring, bears intensely golden yellow daisy-like flowers. Both single and double varieties are available. They go well with red tulips or blue cushion-forming perennials in borders and beds.

Pasque flowers, *Pulsatilla* species, family *Ranunculaceae*, flowering time from the first to second month of spring, are fuzzy beauties that will only grow on permeable, poorish soil. Some species require acid soil. They should never be fertilized.
Warning: these flowers are toxic!

King cups or marsh marigolds
(*Caltha palustris*) belong to the family of *Ranunculaceae,* flower from the second to third month of spring and are easy-to-care-for perennials for the edge of a pond or stream. The soil should contain some lime and plenty of nutrients.
Warning: this plant is toxic!

Primulas are inseparable from the concept of spring. Once the yellow flowers of the wild cowslip appear in the meadows, you know winter is really over.
Botanical name: *Primula* species.
Family: Primulaceae.
Flowering time: early to late spring.
Height: 10-40 cm (4-16 in).
Warning: may cause skin allergies in sensitive people!

Primulas offer a rich variety of shapes and colours.
● Border primulas create colourful clumps of flowers in many brilliant colours, some with contrasting white edges.
● *Primula denticulata*, with its round flowerheads, thrives in moist soil. These plants produce glorious globes of white, violet, pink and red.
● Candelabra primroses can be obtained in strong colours.
● Carpet primulas (*Juliae* hybrids) are also called Carnival primulas. They come in any number of shades from pastel colours to strong, brilliant colours. They proliferate at a fast rate in the garden.
● Auriculas are splendid flowering

beauties that include the Alpine auricula (*Primula auricula*) with its striking golden yellow flower bells.
● The cowslip is a genuine wild primula (*Primula veris*) with scented yellow flowers, while the wild meadow oxlip (*Primula eliator*) bears unscented sulphur yellow flowers.
Primulas look just as good in balcony boxes and bowls as in the garden. The border primulas, in particular, can be planted here late in the spring.
Requirements: sunny to semi-shady position; fresh to moist, humus-rich soil.
Care and planting: undemanding. Short-lived border primulas should be fertilized a little at the time of flowering. Propagate from seed or by division. Plant in the autumn or spring.
Use: flowerbeds, edges of trees, water's edge, bowls and boxes.

Bleeding heart (*Dicentra spectablis*) belongs to the family of *Fumariaceae* and flowers in the last month of spring. It should be planted in a shallow hole in permeable, nutrient-rich soil and then left to grow undisturbed.

Shade-loving herbaceous perennials

Far from living in the gloom, these plants flourish in positions that are shady or semi-shady. Some of them are particularly charming, others are conspicuous for their luxuriant growth.

Many herbaceous plants require the refreshing coolness of the shade for protection against the hot rays of the sun. On the one hand, the sun is a welcome source of warmth, but on the other hand it may burn the sensitive foliage of many plants and dry out the soil too fast, so that the plants quickly die. In the summer, the sun would have an even more lethal effect and heat-sensitive plants would suffer considerably. The effect of the sun is softened in the semi-shade, the soil retains moisture and the temperature differences are not quite so extreme.

Tips on care: The plants introduced here are all easy to grow and care for as long as they are planted in the right positions. The less deep the shade, which means the more light the plant receives, the more moisture is needed in the soil. You might have to water the soil occasionally.

Caucasus forget-me-not and golden strawberry (Duchesnea indica), are two flowers that go well together.

Two species that are reminiscent of forget-me-nots, with tiny, sky-blue flowers, are:

● Blue-eyed Mary (*Omphalodes verna*), family *Boraginaceae*, flowers from mid- to late spring.

● The Caucasus forget-me-not (*Brunnera macrophylla*), family *Boraginaceae*, also flowers from mid- to late spring.

● Both are charming plants for the edge of trees or in the rockery. They quickly form well-developed stands. From mid- to late spring they are covered in a myriad pretty little flowers. These plants are extremely undemanding and require hardly any care at all. It is a good idea to plant the Caucasus forget-me-not under cherry trees. The resulting blue carpet of flowers at the foot of the flowering cherry tree is an unforgettable sight.

Hepatica nobilis has various common names. The leaves appear after the flowers.
Warning: this plant is toxic!

Jerusalem cowslip or lungwort (*Pulmonaria officinalis*). The blue lungwort (*Pulmonaria angustifolia*) has flowers that change colour from pink to blue.

Violets (*Viola* species) like to live modestly in the shade. One of the most popular species is the scented violet (*Viola odorata*) which has a sweet perfume.

Christmas roses (*Helleborus niger*) are some of the first flowers to defy winter. They may flower as early as the first month of winter (around Christmas time in the northern hemisphere), but certainly by the first month of spring. They need an undisturbed position in chalky, humus-rich soil for many years in order to develop properly. Do not fertilize.
Warning: this plant is toxic!

Epimedium species (barrenwort or bishop's hat) are the ballet dancers among the spring flowers. Their other common name of elf flower says much about the graceful attitude of these little flowers, which seem to dance above their beautifully shaped and coloured foliage. Their rhizomes spread rapidly throughout large areas and cover the ground with metallic shiny leaves. Cut back faded foliage.

Other Dicentra species, the sisters of bleeding heart (*D. spectabilis*), look almost as graceful and elegant as the *Epimedium* described left. Whitish, yellow to cherry red flowers, shaped like hearts, cover the plants with their finely slit foliage. The sensitive, rather brittle rootstock has to be handled very carefully when it is planted in shallow, humus-rich soil.

Cushion-forming herbaceous perennials

What would spring be without aubrieta, candytuft etc.? The stunning effect of these plants is created by the multitude of tiny individual flowers which entirely cover the clumps of foliage. Bordering a path or tumbling over the top of a wall, in a rockery or on the edge of a patio, they are one of the wonders of spring.

Alyssum saxatile and *Alyssum montanum* grow about 20 cm (8 in) tall and are covered with golden yellow to sulphur yellow flowers. Their intense scent entices many insects to visit them. They prefer to grow on humus-rich, sandy, stony soil and can be sown straight into the ground where they are intended to grow.

Aubrieta hybrids prefer a sunny, warm position.
Botanical name: *Aubrieta* hybrids.
Family: *Cruciferae.*
Flowering time: mid- to late spring.
Height: about 10 cm (4 in).

Aubrieta deltoidea is one of the most popular cushion-forming perennials. During the middle and last months of spring it flowers in shades of blue, pink or even red.
Requirements: sunny, lime-containing sandy or loamy soil.

Care: always keep the soil sufficiently moist. Only fertilize when in flower. After flowering, cut the cushion back by about a third.

Candytuft shines white to pink in large cushions.
Botanical name: *Iberis sempervirens, Iberis saxatilis.*
Family: *Cruciferae.*
Flowering time: mid- to late spring.
Height: about 10 cm (4 in).

Candytuft owes its name to the colourful white, pink and red shades of its flowers. This bushy little plant is evergreen, so it retains its foliage all year round.
Requirements: cut back after flowering; propagate from cuttings.

NB: *Arabis* species should be included among the cushion-forming perennials. Like the candytufts, they belong to the family *Cruciferae.* In addition to white species and varieties, some pink varieties can now be obtained. The cushions should be divided every two to three years so that they do not deteriorate and become bare from the centre.

Saxifrage or rockfoil (a red species is seen in the photograph above)
Botanical name: *Saxifraga* x *arendsii.*
Family: *Saxifragaceae.*
Flowering time: mid- to late spring.
Height: about 10 cm (4 in).

All shades, from white to pink to red, are produced by the many varieties of saxifrage. Compact cushions, with leaves that are formed out of closely packed individual rosettes, create a closed cover from which 20-cm (8 in) tall, wiry stalks rise up, bearing cup-shaped flowers during the second and third months of spring.
Requirements: light semi-shady, but also fairly sunny, position in humus-rich, loamy to sandy soil.
Care: after flowering, cut off the flower stalks just above the cushion. Fertilize sparingly. Propagate from cuttings in the autumn.

Clouds of forget-me-not surrounding tulips, bleeding heart and saxifrage.

Biennial spring-flowering plants

This section will introduce you to some popular, short-lived, spring-flowering plants. All are suitable for under-planting with bulbous flowers.

Forget-me-not
(Photograph above)
Botanical name: *Myosotis sylvatica.*
Family: *Boraginaceae.*
Flowering time: early to late spring.
Height: 10-40 cm (4-16 in).
The pure, shining blue of the forget-me-not seems to reflect the colour of the sky and will catch the eye in many positions. Clouds of blue flowers are the best kind of setting for brightly coloured tulips but even on a balcony they look wonderful as an accompaniment to other, larger flowers.
Requirements: sunny to semi-shady position; humus-rich soil.
Planting and care: sow seed in early to mid-summer, cover the seed with soil. Prick out the young plants and plant them out in early to mid-autumn. They will need some form of winter protection.

A deep gold wallflower.

Faces full of expression.

White powder-puff daisies.

Wallflower
(Photograph, above)
Botanical name: *Cheiranthus* spp.
Family: *Cruciferae.*
Flowering time: mid- to late spring.
Height: 20-70 cm (8-28 in).
Warning: wallflowers are toxic!

Wallflowers were very popular at one time, although they seem to be less fashionable now. However, the very sweet scent of their yellow, orange or brownish-red flowers still charms gardeners just as it has always done. The present-day selection offers a multitude of colours and sizes. Some varieties grow up to 70 cm (28 in) tall and are very much in demand as cut flowers.
Requirements: sunny to semi-sunny position; nutrient-rich, chalky, humus-rich soil.
Planting and care: cover the seed with soil in the last months of spring, keep an even degree of moisture, then prick out. Plant out the seedlings in early to mid-autumn and give some protection during the winter.
Special note: overwintering can take place in a cold frame, then plant out in the first and second months of spring.

Pansies
(Photograph, above)
Botanical name: *Viola* x *wittrock-iana* hybrids.
Family: *Violaceae.*
Flowering time: early to late spring.
Height: 10-15 cm (4-6 in).

Pansies come in a multitude of shapes and sizes. The early-flowering varieties lift their faces up to the sun from early to late spring; they display the dominant colours of white, yellow and blue. The late varieties (flowering from mid- to late spring) are often multi-coloured, with warmer shades and faces full of expression.
Requirements: sunny to semi-shady position; permeable humus soil, not too rich in nutrients.
Planting and care: sow seed in early to mid-summer, cover with soil, then prick out when ready. Plant out in early to mid- autumn. Do not fertilize.
Use: pansies can be used universally – as an underplanting, as an accompaniment or alone. They are all suited to planting in bowls and boxes; the small-flowered varieties, the miniature pansies, look particularly good in small spaces.

Daisies
(Photograph, above)
Botanical name: *Bellis perennis.*
Family: *Compositae.*
Flowering time: first and second months of spring.
Height: 10-15 cm (4-6 in).

Garden daisies and related species are the cultivated descendants of the plain wild daisy. Their flowers are thickly beset with petals and the individual flowerhead is larger than the wild daisy. Some varieties have flowers resembling small pincushions, others look more like powder puffs. The range of colours extends from pure white to pink to dark red.
Requirements: sunny to semi-shady position; in all soils.
Planting and care: sow seed from late spring to mid-summer, protect the young plants from too much sunlight, then prick out. Plant out from mid-summer. Use bunches of twigs etc. as winter protection.
Special note: ready-bought plants can still be planted in the spring.

Index

Figures in bold indicate illustrations.

Adonis amurensis 52
  vernalis 2, 9, 14, 16, 52, **52**
Alyssum 17, 56, **56**
  montanum 56, **56**
  saxatile 56, **56**
Anemone blanda 51, **51**
  nemorosa 51, **51**
anemones 6, 7, 9, 17, 24, 50, **50**
annuals 6
aphids 20
Arabis 17
Aubrieta 6, 17, 56, **56**
  hybrids 56, **56**
  x *cultorum* 56
autumn, planting in the 28

bacteria 22
bacterial diseases 22
balcony 24
  planting on a 26
balcony boxes 24, 25, 28
  overwintering 30
Bellis perennis 59, **59**
Bergenia 9, 52, **52**
biennials 6, 11
bleeding heart (*Dicentra spectabilis*)
  6, 9, 14, 15, 16, 17, 52, 53, **53**, **58**
blue-eyed Mary (*Omphalodes*) 17, 54
bone chips 12
bonemeal 12
botanical species 9, **10**
botany 6
Botrytis 21, **21**
bowls 25, 26
bringing on plants early 18
Brunnera macrophylla 54, **54**
bulbils 16, 17
  propagation from 17
bulbous iris 6, 21, 49, **49**
  tuber 6
bulbs 6, **6**, 10, 11, 14, 30
  planting in a box **26**
  small 11
Bullesiana hybrids 53
buying plants and bulbs 10, 24, 29

in pots 11

Caltha palustris 53, **53**
candytuft (*Iberis*) 17, 57, **57**
Caucasus forget-me-not (*Brunnera*
  macrophylla) 9, 54, **54**
Cheiranthus cheiri 59, **59**
Chionodoxa 47
  gigantea 47
  luciliae 28, 47
  sardensis 47, **47**
Christmas rose (*Helleborus niger*) 3,
  8, 9, 16, 21, 55, **55**
cold-germinating plants 16
compost 12, 15, 26, 30
containers 25, 26
controlled-release fertilizer 12
cowslip (*Primula veris*) 4, **6**, 28, 52,
  53
Crocus 4, 9, 10, **10**, 11, 12, 17, 18,
  20, **31**, 38, **38**, 39, **45**, **covers**
  albiflorus 39, **39**
  ancyrensis 28, 39, **39**
  angustifolius 39
  chrysanthus 38, 39
  flavus 39
  imperati 39
  sieberi 39
  tomasinianus 9, 39, **39**
  vernus 38, **38**
  versicolor var. *picturatus* 39
cushion perennials 9, 11, 17 56, **56**,
  57, **57**
cushion phlox 17
cutting back 12
cuttings, propagation from 17
Cyclamen 7, 9, 51, **51**
  coum 51
  libanoticum 51
  repandum 51

daffodils 36, **36**, **cover**
daisies (*Bellis*) 24, **25**, 27, **44**, 59,
  59, **cover**
dark-germinating plants 16
Darwin hybrid tulips 35
decay of stem 21, **21**
Dicentra 55, **55**

spectabilis 14, 15, 17, 52, 53, **53**
diseases 19
dog's tooth violet (*Erythronium*
  dens-canis) 9, **10**, 51, **51**
Doronicum 9, 52, **52**
drainage **10**, 11, 26
dry rot 21
dying back 14

Epimedium 55, **55**
Eranthus 43
  cilicica 43
  hyemalis 43, **43**
  x *tubergenii* 43
Erythronia 15, 17
Erythronium 51, **51**
  dens-canis 51
  revolutum 51
  tuolumnense 51, **51**

fern brew 20
fertilizing 12
foliage 15
forget-me-not (*Myosotis*) 4, 13, 16,
  24, **25**, 28, **32-3**, 58, **58**
  Caucasus (*Brunnera macrophylla*)
  54, **54**
Fritillaria 40, **40**, 41, **41**
  acmopetala 40, **41**
  camschatcensis 41
  imperialis 40, **40**
  meleagris 41, **41**
  pallidiflora 41
  persica 41
  raddeana 40
fritillary 9, 10, 15, 40, 41
  "Crown Imperial" 9, **10**, 17, 20,
  40, **40**
  Persian 41
frost 27
  germinating plants 16
  protection from 30
fungal disease 21
Fusarium 21, **21**

Galanthus 10, 42, **42**
  elwesii 42
  nivalis 42, **42**

Index

garden narcissi 9, 36, **36**, **37**
  soil 26
  tulip 9, **10**, 12, 34, **34**, 35, **35**
  varieties 12
garlic brew 20
generative reproduction 16
glory of the snow (*Chionodoxa*) 9, 47, **47**
grape hyacinths (*Muscari botryoides*) 9, **10**, 17, 28, 29, 46, **46**
grey mould 21, **21**

heart flowers (*Dicentra*) 9, 55, **55**
Helleborus 8, 55, **55**
  niger 3, 8, 9, 16, 21, 55, **55**
Hepatica nobilis 8, 55, **55**
hoop petticoat narcissi 15, 37
humidity 8
humus, bark 26
hyacinth 9, **10**, 17, 18, 21, 44, **44**, 45, **45**
  Spanish 47, **47**
  wood 47
Hyacinthoiodes non-scripta 47
Hyacinthus orientalis 44, **44**, 45, **45**

Iberis 17, **57**
  saxatilis 57
  sempervirens 57
insecticide 19
Iris 9, 48, **48**, 49, **49**
  barbata "Nana" 49, **49**
  bearded 32-3, 49, **49**
  bucharica 48, **48**
  bulbous 48, 49
  danfordiae 48
  dwarf 49
  graebneriana 48
  histrio 48
  histrioides 48
  reticulata 10, 49, **49**

jonquils 15, 29
Juliae hybrids 53

Kaufmann tulips 9
leaf burn 21

Leucojum vernum 10, 43, **43**
light 8
  -germinating plants 16
lungwort (*Pulmonaria officinalis*) 16, 55, **55**

mare's tail brew 20
marsh marigold (*Caltha palustris*) 9, 17, **22-3**, 53, **53**
mildew 20, 21
Multiflora hyacinths 45
Muscari armeniacum 46, **46**
  botryoides 46
  comosum 46
  neglectum 46
mycosis 21
Myosotis sylvatica 4, 58, **58**

names, botanical 7
narcissi 4, 9, 10, **10**, 11, 12, 17, 20, 21, 24, **36**, 37, **37**
  angel's tears 36
  cup 36
  cyclamineus 9, 29, **31**, 37
  double 36
  garden 36
  hoop petticoat 37
  jonquil 37
  orchid-flowered 37
  Poetaz 37
  Poeticus **22-3**, **32**, 37, **37**
  scented 37
  split-corona 37
  Tazetta 37
  Triandus 36
  trumpet **22-3**, 24, 36
Narcissus 10, 36, **36**, 37, **37**
  bulbocodium 15, 37
  fire 21
  fly **21**
  pseudonarcissus 9
nematodes 20, 21, **21**
nettle brew 12, 20
nutrients 12

Omphalodes verna 17, 54
overfertilizing 12
overwintering 30

oxlip (*Primula elatior*) 53

pansies 6, 12, 16, 24, 27, 28, 29, 59, **59**
pasque flower (*Pulsatilla*) 9, 14, 16, 52, **52**
perennials 6, **6**, 9, 10, 11, **11**, 14, 17, 24, 27, 30, 52, **52**, 53, **53**, 54, **54**, 55, **55**, 56, **56**
  dividing 17
  small 24
pests 19
pH factor 8
pheasant's eye (*Adonis vernalis*) 2, 9, 14, 16, 52, **52**
plant container 26
  sprays, biological 20
  supports 27
planting 10, 11
  autumn 26
  basket 11, **11**
  compost 26
  depths **10**, 11, 26
  out 16
  spacing 25
  spring 27
  times 10, 11, 28
plants 6, 25, 27, **27**
  choosing 24
  nutrients 12
  protection agents 19
Poeticus narcissi 9, 37, **37**
pricking out 16
Primula 6, 9, 16, 21, 28, **44**, 52, 53, **53**
  auricula 28, 52, 53
  bullesiana hybrids 53
  denticulata 28
  elatior 53
  veris 4, 28, 52, 53
  vulgaris hybrids
primulas, carpet 53
  cushion 28, 29, 53
  globe 53
propagation 8, 16, 17
Pulmonaria officinalis **55**, 56
Pulsatilla 14, 52, **52**
Ranunculus 9, **10**, 17, 28, 50, **50**

Index

asiaticus 50, **50**
reproduction, non-sexual 16
  vegetative 16
rockery 9
root rot 21
rooting in compost 17
  in water 17

Saxifraga x *arendsii* 57, **57**
saxifrage 16, 57, **57**, **58**
Scilla 9, 10, 12, 16, 21, **31**, 46, **46**,
  47, **47**
  bifolia 46
  siberica 28, 46, **46**
seed, propagation from 16
shade-loving perennials 54, **54**, 55,
  55
slugs and snails 20
snake's head fritillary (*Fritillaria
  meleagris*) 9, 12, 41, **41**
snowdrop (*Galanthus*) 9, 10, **10**, 16,
  21, 42, **42**
snowflake (*Leucojum vernum*) 9, 10,
  14, 43, **43**
soil 8
  analysis 8, 12, 63
  consistency 8
  improvement 12, 30
  preparation 10
sowing seed 16
spacing of plants 11
species, botanical 7
spring, planting in 10, 28
stem rot 21
storing bulbs and tubers 15
sun-loving perennials 52, **52**, 53, **53**

Tazetta narcissi 18, **37**
thrips 20
trace elements 12
Triteleia laxa **9**, **47**
tubers 6, **7**, 10, 11, 14, **17**, 30
  new 16
  propagation from 17
tulip fire 21
Tulipa 24, 28, 35, **46**
  kaufmanniana 24, 36, **46**
  praestans "Fuselier" 28

sylvestris 35
tarda 35
tulips 4, 6, 11, 20, 21, 24, **24**, **27**,
  34, **34**, 35, **35**, **45**, **58**
  botanical 9, **10**, 35
  Chamaeleon 22
  cottage 24, 35
  Darwin 13, 24, 35
  double late 9, 35
  early 34, **34**
  Fosteriana 35
  Greigii 35, **35**
  Kaufmann 24, 35, **46**
  late 25, 35, **35**
  lily-flowered 35, **35**, **cover**
  medium early 34, **34**
  parrot 2, **32-3**, 35
  peony-flowered 24
  Rembrandt 22, 35
  single early 24, **34**
  Viridiflora **19**, 35, **35**
  water lily 24, 29, 35
  Weinberg 35
  wild **31**

Viola 9, 16, 55, **55**
  cornuta 28
  odorata 55
  x *wittrockiana* hybrids 28, 59, **59**
violets 9, 16, 55, **55**
  scented 55, **55**
viral disease 22
virosis 21, **21**, 22

wallflower (*Cheiranthus cheiri*) 6, 21,
  24, **25**, 59, **59**
watering 12, 27
waterlogging 11
wet rot 21
windflowers (wood anemone) 51, **51**
winter aconite (*Eranthis*) 6, **7**, 9, **10**,
  11, 16, 43, **43**, 46
  protection 15, 31
wood hyacinth 47

Having your soil analysed

If you wish to have a soil analysis made, you will have to submit a sample of mixed soil. Choose several spots in the garden and, using a spade, take specimens from a depth of 20-30 cm (8-12 in). You can take a smaller specimen by scraping soil off the blade of the spade with a spoon. The individual specimens should be mixed up thoroughly in a bucket. About 300-500 g (10-18 oz) of soil, without any large roots or stones, can be sent for analysis in a plastic bag. Enquire at your local garden centre for the address of a laboratory that will provide a soil analysis for you.

Author's note

This book is concerned with the care of spring flowers. Some of the species described here (the entire plant including bulbs/tubers) are more or less toxic! The section of the book giving descriptions of the plants (pp. 32-59) points out which plants are toxic. You must make absolutely sure that children and pets do not eat any part of these plants. Some of the plants also secrete substances which may irritate your skin. If you have sensitive skin or suffer from contact allergies, you should make sure that you wear gloves when handling these plants. If you suffer an open cut or other injury while working with soil, visit your doctor to discuss the possibility of having a tetanus injection! All fertilizers and plant protection agents, even the organic or biological ones, should be stored in a place that is inaccessible to children and pets. These agents should not be allowed to come into contact with your eyes. If you are preparing large vats or containers of herbal brew (for spraying etc.), cover the top of the container so that small children or animals cannot climb in.

Cover photographs
Front cover: *Daffodils (trumpet narcissi).*
Inside front cover: *Crocuses.*
Inside back cover: *Lily-flowered tulips and daisies.*
Back cover: *Crocuses on the lawn.*

Photographic acknowledgements
Apel: p. 51 bottom left; Becker: inside front cover/1, 22/23, 32/33, 34 right, 55 top centre, 64/inside back cover; Borstell: p. 2 bottom, 24, 35 top left; de Cuveland: p. 53 bottom right; IfB: p. 46 top; Köhlein: p. 48, 49; Laux: p. 37 top, 39 bottom, 41 right, 46 bottom, 51 top right, 52 bottom right, 55 bottom centre; Layer: p. 4, 39 top, 41 left, 59 centre; Nickig: p. 9, 13, 14, 18, back cover; Pforr: p. 3; Reinhard: p. 37 bottom, 38, 40 top, 43 right, 50, 51 top left, 52 bottom left, 53 top left, 54, 55 top left, 55 top right, 57 right, 59 right; Ruckszio: p. 42, 43 left, 47 left, 52 top left, 55 bottom left; Sammer: p. 8, 19, 35 bottom left, 40 bottom, 53 top right, 55 bottom right, 56 right, 57 left, 59 left; Seidl: p. 51 top centre; Silvestris/Kuch: p. 36; Silvestris/Layer: front cover, 52 top right; Silvestris/NHPA: p. 5; Scherz: p. 2 top, 32; Strauss: p. 25, 31, 44, 45, 47 top right, bottom right, 51 bottom right, 56 right, 58.

This edition published 1994 by
Merehurst Limited
Ferry House, 51-57 Lacy Road,
Putney, London SW15 1PR

© 1989 Gräfe und Unzer GmbH, Munich

ISBN 1 85391 332 4

A catalogue record for this book is available from the British Library.

English text copyright ©
Merehurst Limited 1994
Translated by Astrid Mick
Edited by Lesley Young
Design and typesetting by
Cooper Wilson Design
Illustrations by György Jankovics
Printed in Italy by Canale & C.S.p.A.